Waveney Walks

Exploring the Norfolk – Suffolk Border

John Arnett

First published 2023
© 2023 John Arnett

Reproduction of all or any part of this publication is not permitted in any form, including print, photocopy, electronic, computer application or on the Internet, without written permission of the copyright holder.

John Arnett has asserted his moral right under the Copyright, Designs and Patents Act 1988 to be identified as the author of this work.

While every effort has been made to ensure the accuracy of the information in this book, John Arnett can accept no responsibility for changes to locations, footpaths and other routes after the publication of it. The existence of a path in this book does not imply that there is a public right of way.

Walkers undertake the walks in this book at their own risk and no responsibility can be accepted by John Arnett for any accident or other event resulting from the use of this book.

ISBN 978 1 84674 416 7

Photographs: front cover – Burgh St Peter Staithe, back cover – Riverside, Beccles, this page – Wardley Hill

Produced through Countryside Books
Designed and Typeset by KT Designs, St Helens
Printed by Holywell Press, Oxford

Contents

Introduction – Spirit of Place (*and Key to maps*)   6

ONE Source to Harleston

1.	Thelnetham Windmill and Little Ouse Fens	9
2.	Wortham Ling	12
3.	Thornham Magna	16
4.	Oakley and Dove Valley	19
5.	Hoxne Treasures	22
6.	Syleham, Brockdish and Angles Way	26

TWO Harleston to Bungay

7.	Harleston – town and country	30
8.	Redenhall and Wortwell	34
9.	Withersdale Street	37
10.	Wortwell Mill and Limbourne Common	40
11.	Alburgh – Holbrook Hill	43
12.	St. Peter, South Elmham	46
13.	Earsham Mill and Marshes	49

THREE Bungay to Beccles

14.	Wainford Maltings	54
15.	Mettingham Castle	57
16.	Ilketshall St. Andrew and St. John	60
17.	Ellingham Mill and Wardley Hill	63
18.	Ringsfield	66
19.	Geldeston – byways and waterways	69

Contents (continued)

FOUR Beccles to the Coast

20.	Chedgrave Common and Wherrymans Way	73
21.	Dunburgh and Beccles Riverside	76
22.	Burgh St Peter and Carlton Marshes	79
23.	Herringfleet Hills and Somerleyton Staithe	82
24.	St Olaves and Waveney Forest	86
25.	Oulton Marshes Nature Reserve	90

Recommended Reading, Maps and Useful Organisations   94

Acknowledgements   96

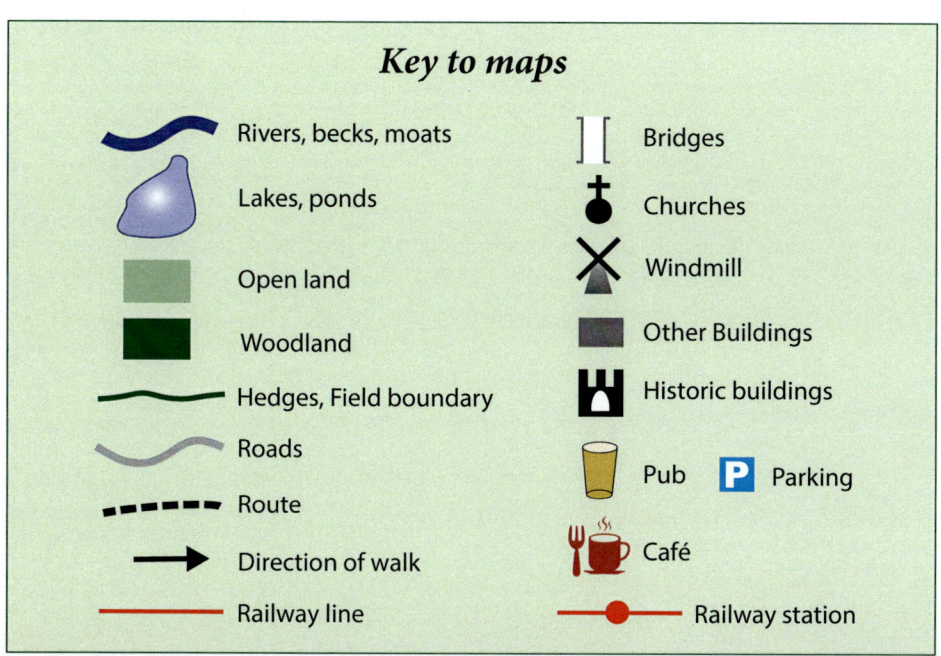

Introduction – Spirit of Place

The unifying theme of this collection of walks is the River Waveney and its very appealing and characterful lowland valley. From its source in the fens of the East to its mature seaward destination via the expansive estuary of Breydon Water near Great Yarmouth, the river is the guiding spirit. The walks are divided into four sections, from West to East, as the river broadens and advances. Many include riverside stretches, nearly all are circular and each highlights a distinctive aspect of this fascinating region, on the border between Norfolk and Suffolk, the river itself marking the boundary. Some of the walks are in Norfolk, some are in Suffolk, some are in both.

The walks have been purposely designed and arranged to highlight the surprising diversity of landscape, natural features, settlements, historic buildings, bridges and crossings associated with the working river at its different stages. There is a great deal in the locality to capture the imagination, from all periods and to suit a diversity of interests. To give just a few examples – maritime heritage, major archaeological finds of all periods, commons and marshes, castle ruins, a superb Saxon shore fort, water and wind mills, a heated riverside lido, an abundance of medieval round tower churches, and a multitude of historic and relatively unspoilt market towns and villages. It is a region that often feels like a very well kept secret, where the pace of change has been comparatively slow. From Bungay, eastward to the coast, the river marks the southern edge of the Broads National Park, the smallest of the UK's fifteen national parks, but its 4th most visited. This brings with it the many watery attractions for which the Broads are famous – sailing, canoeing, cruising, pleasure boats, angling.

The very evocative name "Waveney" is Saxon in origin, the word "wafien" meaning waving or turbulent waters, the suffix "en" denoting a river. The sight of waving reeds along its banks is guaranteed to bring this to mind. The river has its source at Lopham and Redgrave Fen, Suffolk, and reaches the sea, almost 60 miles later, at the very historic South Quay waterfront of Great Yarmouth, Norfolk (a fascinating walk in itself, full of reminders of the town's maritime importance). Eastwards from Geldeston, near Beccles, the river is both tidal and navigable. The Waveney's average elevation, along its course, is 31 metres or just over 100 ft. above sea level.

All rivers are, of course, a major feature in the landscape, and all have been associated with certain functions regardless of time or place. These include being sources of water and of food, being used for transport, for driving machinery, for bathing and swimming, for borders, for defence and for disposal of waste. (The last is very topical, in the light of current concerns nationally about water quality.) All of these are or have been true of the River Waveney. Suffice to say, walking is, quite simply the perfect and indeed the prototype mode of travel, and the perfect pace at which to appreciate the myriad moods and pleasures of the Waveney Valley – and of course, to really get to know a place you have to go on foot.

On a personal note, many of these walks were first conceived and plotted out in the spring and summer of 2020, during the first lockdown. The spring weather was exceptionally sunny and warm, and to be able to escape on successive days, walking and exploring with a notebook, an OS map and a flask of coffee, seemed like an extraordinary privilege and pleasure in those very constrained times. Often I wouldn't see another person. It was, and continues to be, the best kind of therapy, along with all the proven physical benefits of this most timeless form of outdoor exercise.

The walks vary in length from 2 to 4 ½ miles, and some can easily be extended or combined. Features of interest are briefly explained in the notes for each walk, along with a note about what kind of terrain and walking conditions to expect as well as details of nearby facilities and eateries. Not all walkers will be motorists, but the walks generally start in places where parking is easily available; where this is not obvious, I have suggested where to park. The further reading section at the end of the book gives details of relevant reference and other books on the Waveney Valley and wider area, and details of writers associated with it, from different periods, as well as useful local organisations, for those who wish to explore further.

NB Because many of these walks are in low-lying areas of river valley, robust waterproof footwear is essential. This is especially the case in the winter months when the land and footpaths are often waterlogged. For this reason also, the walks are not generally suitable for wheelchair users. Distances are approximate.

Abbreviations used in the text

FP	Footpath	GR	Grid reference
RHS	Right hand side	PC	Postcode
LHS	Left hand side	C	Century
Yds	Yards	SSSI	Site of Special Scientific Interest

ONE
Source to Harleston

Ocean Pit, Harleston

# 1. *Thelnetham Windmill and Little Ouse Fens*

This walk takes in the very attractive and varied landscapes of the headwaters of the Little Ouse, including Blo Norton, Thelnetham and Hinderclay Fens. It features undulating, unspoilt countryside, with riverside footpaths and boardwalks, fenland and woods, wayside sculptures and a splendid historic windmill.

Distance 3 miles, inc. extension.
Terrain Fens and riverside can be very boggy. Waterproof footwear is essential. Very minor roads, marked footpaths, section of Angles Way, boardwalk.
Refreshments The recently refurbished White Horse, South Lopham and The Cross Keys, Redgrave are both historic village pubs with dining.

MAP OS Explorer 230
GR   TM010789
PC   IP22 1JS

START

The walk begins at Thelnetham Windmill very close to the sources of both the Waveney *(1), flowing East and the Little Ouse, flowing West. The windmill lies between the villages of Thelnetham and Blo Norton, to the West of Diss, off the A1066. You can park on the green facing the windmill. *(2)

Facing the windmill, turn right and follow the minor road for a short way towards Blo Norton. Just before the bridge and by a wooden sculpture and information boards, go right through a gate and into Parkers Piece *(3). Follow the riverside path here, alongside the youthful Little Ouse, until you come to a wooden bridge, with another sculpture and information boards. Cross over the bridge and carry on, with the river on your right now. After a while the path becomes a boardwalk.

When you come to a second wooden bridge, cross over into Thelnetham Fen. Follow the path, which before long turns away from the river, at right angles to it, for 150 yards or so, before turning left again on a grassy track towards woods. When you reach the woods, cross over a wooden bridge with FP and Angles Way signs. Keep ahead on this wooded path/track through mature trees, soon with a fence and farmland to your RHS. Before long you will be in Hinderclay

Thelnetham Windmill

Fen – see another information board/carving for information about the fen. You will see beautiful yellow gorse flowers here in spring, on the heathland.

When you come to a crossroads of tracks, with arrow signs, you have a choice. 1) you can do a shortish extension by carrying on straight ahead at the crossroads on the Angles Way, across a very pleasant open stretch of heathland to a metal footbridge across the river, and then back the same way to the "crossroads". Total distance about ½ mile. This way you get to see the whole of Hinderclay Fen before returning. Or 2) Turn left at the crossroads and head uphill across a large field towards a farmhouse (Wymers Farm) with paddocks. Turn left at the road and follow it, as it winds its way back, passing Thatchers, Honeysuckle and Lilac cottages on your right. In either case you will return as described in option 2.

Opposite Lilac Cottage take a path off to your left (Willie's Walk) into the woods and Blo Norton Fen *(4). This soon becomes a boardwalk, leading back to the river. When you get to the river, turn right. You can cross either of the two bridges to return alongside the river to the starting point, with the windmill now visible ahead.

NOTES
1. The River Waveney rises in nearby Redgrave and Lopham Fen. This is a national nature reserve and SSSI, and is the largest remaining river valley fen in England. It has a variety of waymarked walks, of different lengths, as well

as a Suffolk Wildlife Trust visitor centre and carpark on Low Common Rd, IP22 2HX. Entrance is free. The Little Ouse is 37 miles in length, and flows in the opposite direction to the Waveney, west to Thetford and beyond.

2. The very attractive landmark of Thelnetham Windmill was built in 1819, and operated successfully throughout the C19th. By 1926 however, it had become derelict. It was restored in the 1980s by a group of volunteers. It is one of only four such restored mills in Suffolk.

3. Parkers Piece (echoes of Cambridge here…) is an area of land adjacent to the upper reaches of the Little Ouse. It is owned and managed by the Little Ouse Headwaters Project (LOHP), a proactive community conservation project. It was set up in 2002 to re-establish a continuous corridor of wildlife habitat along this stretch of the river.

4. The first record of the unusual prefix "Blo" being added to the name Norton, is in 1291. In Middle English it may have meant "bleak" or "exposed". The village is on the Norfolk side of the border.

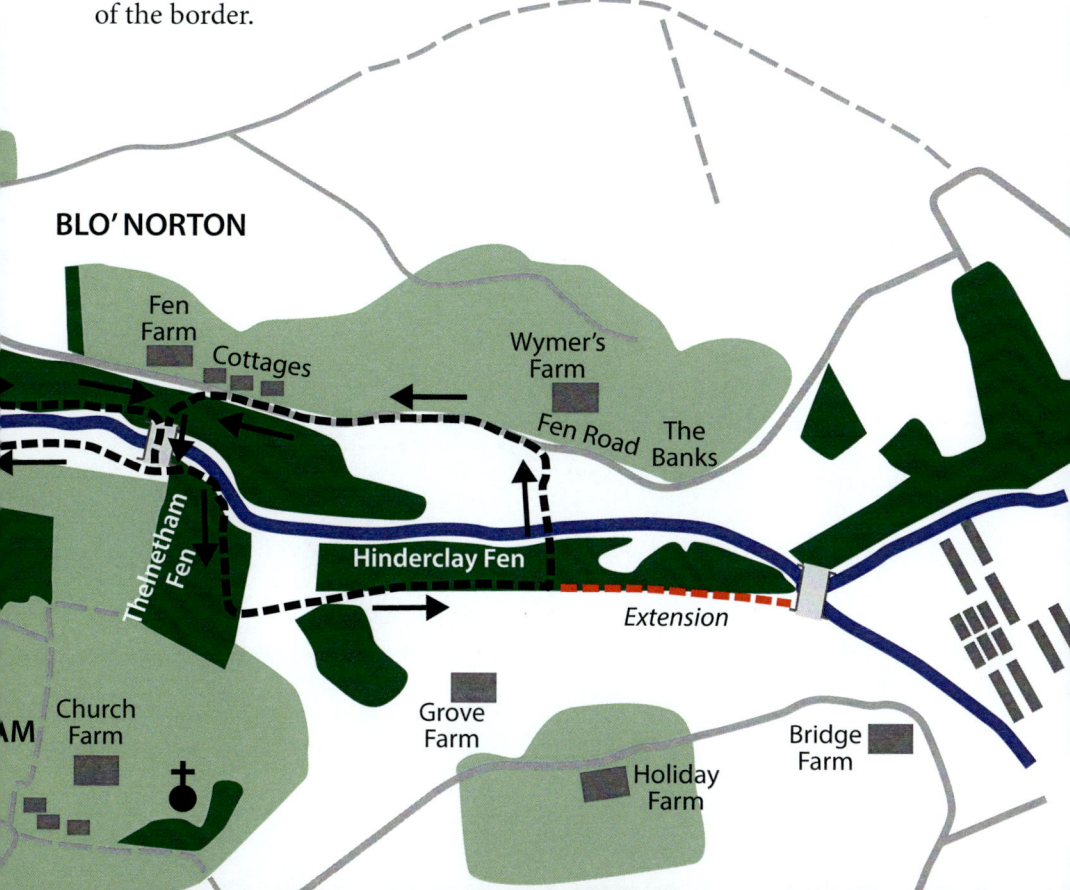

2. Wortham Ling

A walk that explores the unique ecological enclave that is Wortham Ling, with its very pleasing and distinctive flora, landscape and scattered pattern of settlement. The route passes through the beautiful churchyard of St Mary the Virgin, with its mighty round tower.

Distance 2½ miles.

Terrain Signed footpaths, including section of Angles Way, and minor roads.

Refreshments Fair Green, Diss: The Angel Café; The Cock Inn – 1 mile from starting point. Both feature pleasant outdoor seating areas on the green, which is an attraction in itself, especially in summer. The White Hart in neighbouring Roydon is also a beautifully situated pub, next to the church of St Remigius, and with a large outdoor seating area and covered patio, affording fine far reaching views.

MAP   OS Explorer 230
GR   TM094789
PC   IP22 1SP

START

The common, near the Anglia Autoflow works, on Wortham Ling *1. There is a group of buildings and houses spaced around the common here – take the FP by a high hedge to the right of a tall, three storey house, The Homestead (shown on OS map). This path leads straight across the middle of a large field – how well defined it is will depend on the time of year/crop. At the far end you will see a wooden gate in the hedge. Go through, bearing right around the perimeter of this next field.

Half way along the second side of this field you will see a gate with a FP arrow. Follow this around the edge of the next field towards a metal gate at a crossroads, with a sign. Take a right turn here, signposted "Wortham Church and Mellis". Stay on this road (Wigwam Hill) for about ½ mile, past the grand Wortham House and Coach House, heading downhill. At the bottom of the hill, before the junction, turn right at an Angles Way FP sign into the beautiful churchyard of St. Mary's Wortham *(2). The church has a remarkably broad and imposing Norman round tower, open to one side.

WORTHAM LING 13

Skirt round the back of the church and downwards (beware of nettles here) to a kissing gate, and then across a small field to a second pair of gates. Cross the field diagonally left to more gates, then taking the right hand path into woods. Here, the path divides – turn right, heading uphill. At the top keep straight ahead, directly across the middle of a field. At the far end of the field, keep straight ahead down the side of a thatched house (there is a right of way here) to join a road, Rectory Rd.

Turn left at the road, following it downhill past the attractive curved terrace of Rash Crescent on your left, followed by some more houses, to a junction. Turn right here, after White House and Fox Cottage (signposted "Palgrave and Diss") still on Rectory Rd, which goes across the middle of Wortham Ling. For this final stretch you can usually walk alongside rather than actually on the road. Ignore a track to your right and keep straight ahead to a junction.

Turn right here (also signed "Palgrave and Diss") on Ling Rd. After a few hundred yards, just beyond a sign for Riverside House, turn right once more at a sign for Anglia Autoflow, now on Low Water Lane. Here it is worth pausing to read the information board about Wortham Ling SSSI

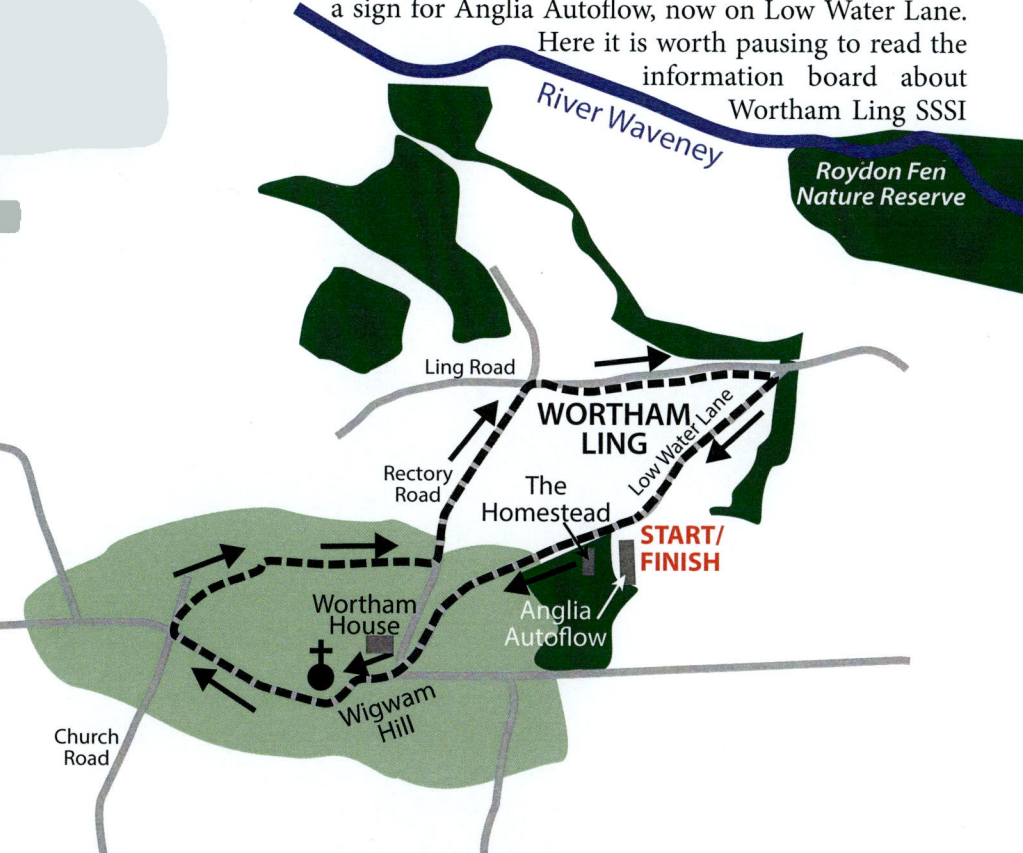

14 SOURCE TO HARLESTON

Diss Mere, winter

and the common. Follow this road for just over ¼ mile back to the starting point.

NOTES
1. Wortham Ling. The word "ling" is simply another name for heather. Wortham Ling is a common, and a SSSI, on account of its distinctive and ecologically valuable lowland heath flora and fauna. The soil is sandy, acidic and very dry.

Wortham Ling heather

The heather comes into spectacular flower in late summer and is home to solitary bees, which unlike honey and bumblebees, as the name suggests, don't live in colonies. In spring, yellow gorse is in flower; in early summer, rusty red sheeps sorrel and white heath bedstraw flowers give a different colour palette to the undergrowth. Other characteristic species include the common lizard, willow warbler, chiffchaff and whitethroat – see information boards for details.
2. The church of St Mary the Virgin was built in the C12th. It has an ancient tower, possibly of C11th origin, built of flint, and now roofless. At 9 metres across, it is the largest diameter round tower church in England. Interestingly, it is shown on the OS map as "Watchtower (remains of)".

In the vicinity… Wortham Ling, and Fair Green, are on the outskirts of the South Norfolk market town of Diss. Once you get beyond the urban sprawl of Victoria Rd, the historic centre (including the "Heritage Triangle" conservation area) is a pleasure to explore on foot, with its shops, amenities and historic buildings of all periods. There are plenty of green spaces to stop and relax, particularly around the 6 acre Mere, reputedly the second deepest lake in England and the focal point of the town. Mere St, the main shopping street, is pedestrianised by day, and leads up to the landmark church of St Mary. Beyond the church, Mount St is an unspoilt and diverse architectural delight. The recently restored and reinvigorated Corn Hall on nearby St Nicholas St is a thriving arts centre and venue, with café, bar, concert hall and exhibition spaces, and is a useful source of local information.

3. Thornham Magna

Located in the extensive and beautifully wooded Thornham estate in the Dove Valley of North Suffolk, this charming walk traverses fields, meadows and ancient woodlands, returning through the very attractive village on a footpath by the stream.

Distance 2 miles.
Terrain Marked footpaths, permissive path, minor roads, path through village.
Refreshments The Four Horseshoes pub in the village has a large restaurant and beer garden (see note). Alternatively, the Forge Café is adjacent to the Thornham Walks Visitor Centre and car park.

MAP OS Explorer 230
GR   TM103711
PC   IP23 8HB

START

The Street, Thornham Magna *(1) by the Street Forge Workshops and red telephone box (which now houses a great selection of books). On the same side, you will see a green FP sign. Take this path, along the edge of a field with a stream bordered by mature trees to your right. Follow this till you come to a junction, close to a road (the entrance to Thornham Walks car parks, visitor centre and café is 150 yds further along this road).

Take the permissive path to your left, passing a sign saying "Bramley Cottage and Gull Lane Cottage only". Carry on past Bramley Cottage, and when you reach a clearing by Gull Lane Cottage, take the path into woods to RHS, up 6 steps. Stay on this path, keeping straight ahead, out of the woods and across a field, with a row of trees on your left. You will pass a detached house on LHS as you head towards woods. Keep ahead into the woods, and turn left almost immediately, soon passing a pond on your right. Stay straight ahead on this path, past hedges and gardens, to a road. You are now back on The Street, but further down.

Edinburgh Belt

New Wood

THORNHAM MAGNA **17**

Turn right and head down to the crossroads, where you will see The Four Horseshoes pub *(2) on your right. Cross over and carry straight on onto Water Lane. After 100 yards or so, at a sign for The Water House and by a marker post, turn right on a green track between hedges. Soon the path turns sharp left and down towards a wooden bridge over the River Dove. Once across the bridge, carry straight ahead on the path, which at first has a fence and meadow

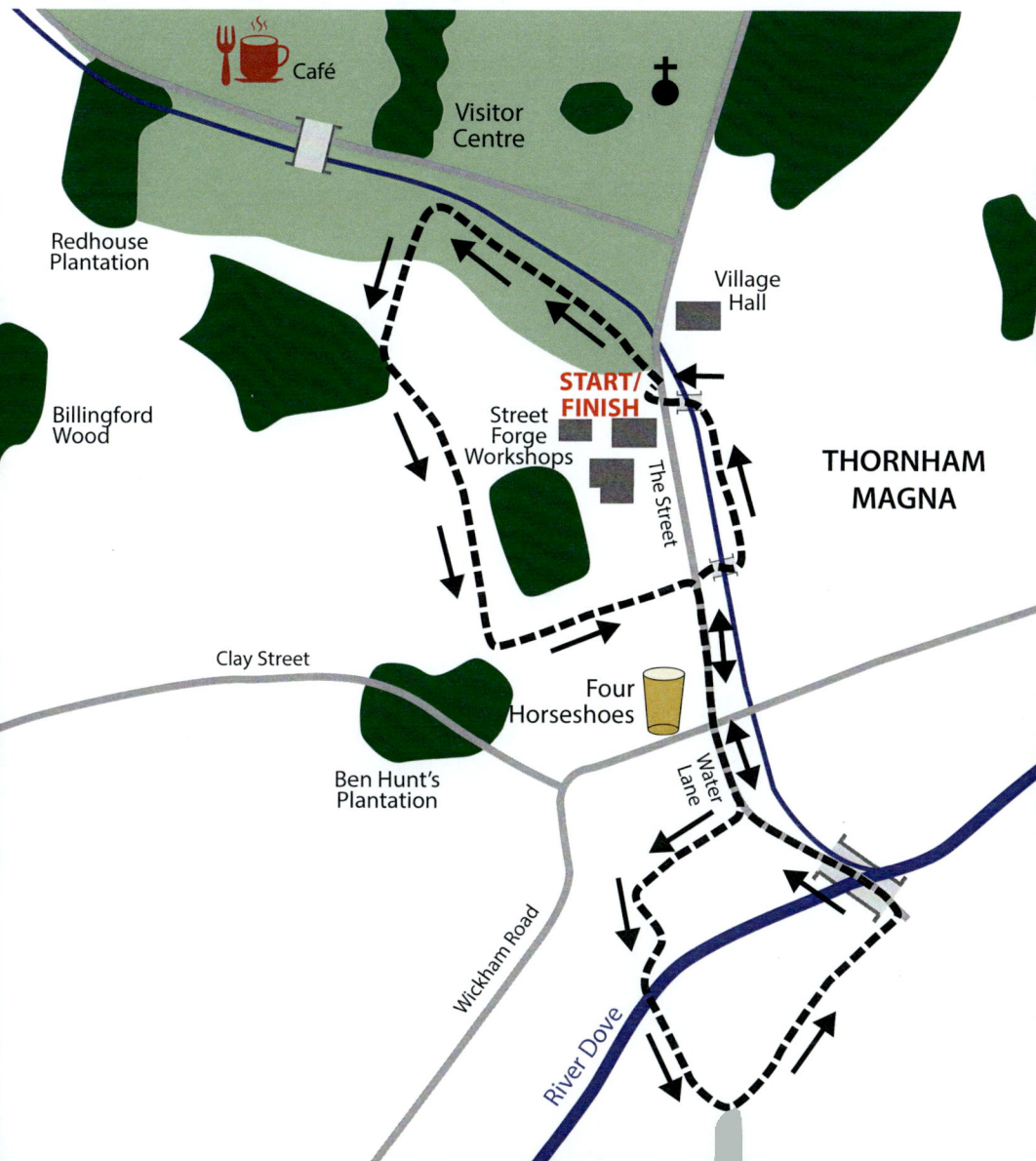

18 SOURCE TO HARLESTON

Thornham Magna, Four Horseshoes

to your LHS and then becomes more enclosed, with hedges and low trees to both sides. When you come to a wooden gate, go through and left, and then left again through another gate.

You will now be on a broader, tree-lined path with green and white waymarker posts. When you reach another gate, by a FP sign, keep straight ahead and cross the stream by a wooden bridge and ford, close to a house. Turn left then, back onto Water Lane, and follow the lane back to the crossroads at The Four Horseshoes. Cross over, back onto The Street. Carry on up The Street, and when you reach a metal bridge by Little St. Farm (opposite where the FP came out earlier) you can join the FP that runs between the stream and the row of picturesque housefronts, heading back to the starting point.

NOTES

1. The two villages of Thornham Magna and its smaller counterpart Thornham Parva, a mile away, lie within the 2,000 acres of park, farm and woodland that make up the Thornham Estate. The estate is situated in the Dove Valley of North Suffolk, the Dove being a tributary of the Waveney. It boasts 11 miles of permissive walks – The Thornham Walks – created in the early 1980s by the late Lord Henniker and his wife, Julia. Since the 1990s the Walks have been managed in a partnership agreement with Suffolk County Council and Mid Suffolk District Council. Thornham Hall houses, in addition to a farm, a number of other enterprises, a walled garden, a gallery, a restaurant and café. Thornham Parva is well worth a visit also, for its exceptionally beautiful C12th thatched church (St. Mary's).

2. The spacious and atmospheric thatched C15th Thornham Magna pub, The Four Horseshoes, should not be missed either. It has accommodation, a sizeable restaurant area as well as outdoor seating, open fires and even a well, in the main bar.

4. Oakley and Dove Valley

Off the beaten track certainly, this walk has plenty of interest and variety – some very attractive open views of parkland, countryside and river valley, grand country houses, picturesque cottages and a handsome, isolated church.

> **Distance** 2½ miles.
> **Terrain** Marked footpaths, tracks, minor roads.
> **Refreshments** The Oaksmere is a country house hotel, restaurant and bar set in 17 acres of parkland, in nearby Brome. Alternatively, the towns of Diss and Eye, each about 2 ½ miles away, have a good range of cafés and pubs.
>
> **MAP**   OS Explorer 230
> **GR**   TM157773
> **PC**   IP21 4BW

START

Car park at church of St Nicholas, Oakley *(1) SE of Diss. Turn right out of the car park and walk down Church Lane for about a third of a mile. Turn left when you come to a junction at the Brome and Oakley parish sign. After about 100 yards, having passed Poppy Cottage and the Barn House, turn right at a triangular green by a yew hedge and large white detached house (Oakley House). Carry on walking down this tree-lined avenue with broad grassy verges. Where the road divides, at houses, bear slightly right on a track with sign for the Old Mill. Follow this track, which soon curves round to the right, towards woods.

At this point you can take a short and very pleasant digression (recommended) of 10/15 minutes, there and back, down to the River Dove *(2). At a post with several FP signs, go straight ahead alongside a fence. Follow this grassy, tree-lined cart track, with banks on either side and views of the picturesque and surprisingly deep Dove valley to your right. At the bottom of the hill, where the track turns right at two gateposts, keep straight ahead by a fence, following a Mid Suffolk FP sign. After taking in the view at a largish wooden bridge over the River Dove, a green and pleasant enclave, re-trace your steps to the top.

Back at the post with the various FP signs, turn left, with wind turbines visible in the distance. Follow this gravelly track skirting fields, with woods to your LHS.

Where the track turns left, keep straight ahead, following the FP sign, between woods and field. At the top of this field turn right into the next, following the sign, and with a field on your left now. Ignore FP signs into the woods, and carry on. Where the trees run out, turn right at a gap, along the edge of a field, towards a white cottage with pantile roof. Go through a gap in the hedge, at the corner of this field, out onto a road. Turn left here.

Shortly after passing the cottage (Rose Farm) you will see a FP sign on your right, opposite a 40mph sign. Follow this path round (may be overgrown!) until it opens out and follows the right hand edge of a large field. Stay on this path, with turbines ahead to your left. At the end of the field, turn right, passing a pond and making sure the hedge is to your left. This path soon becomes enclosed, and shortly emerges at the lychgate of St Nicholas Oakley, your starting point.

NOTES
1. St Nicholas, Oakley occupies a very secluded and tranquil setting on the South (Suffolk) side of the Waveney. It is one of those churches, quite

Oakley, River Dove

OAKLEY AND DOVE VALLEY

common in this part of the country, which appear to be altogether remote and distanced from the village they serve. The square tower is early C14th, and the exterior mostly flint-knapped.

2. The River Dove is tributary of the Waveney, and is 15 miles in length. It rises near Hoxne, and passes through Eye and Thornham Magna before joining the Waveney near Homersfield.

In the vicinity ... The church of St Mary in the neighbouring village of Brome, is of great interest too, with its verdant rural setting, ancient, partly Saxon round tower, copious stained glass, and array of medieval Cornwallis family tombs. The interior has a striking feeling of antiquity, despite (or perhaps because of) extensive Victorian restoration.

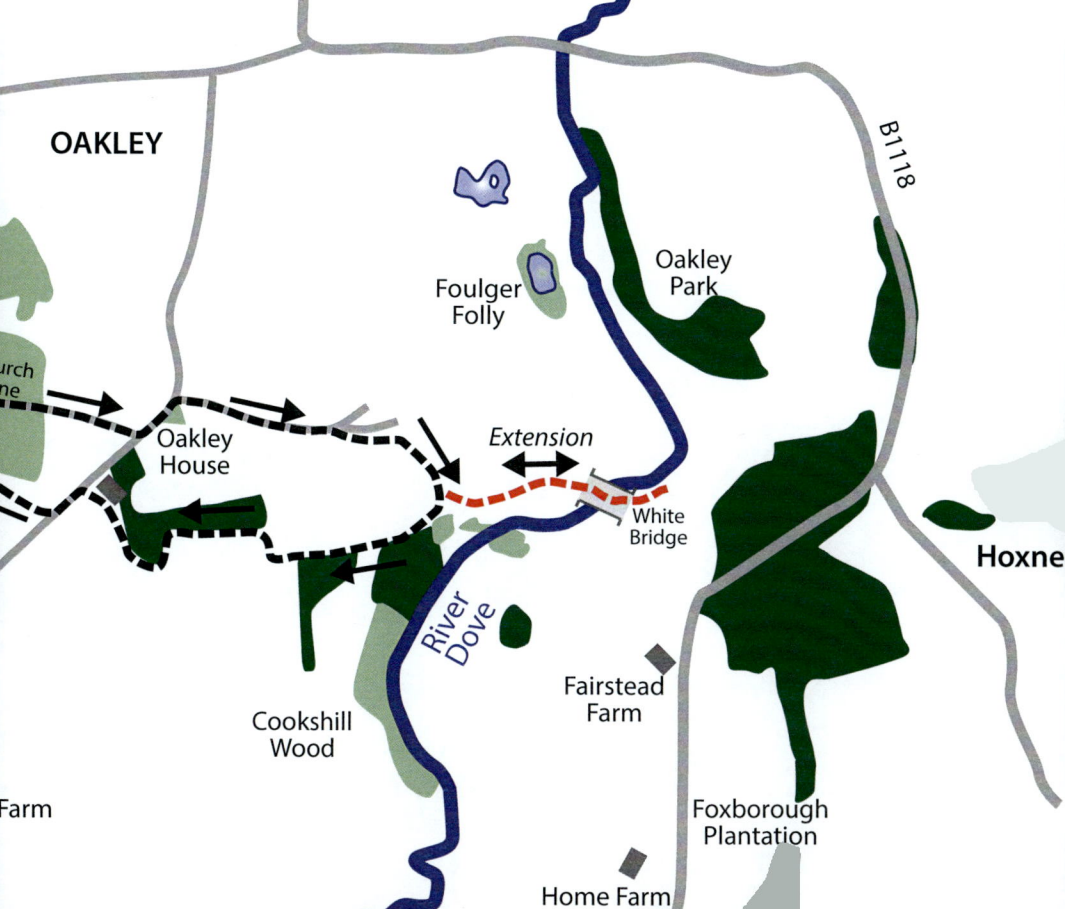

5. *Hoxne Treasures*

Hoxne is a remarkable and historic village in many ways and for diverse reasons. This walk, starting from the very attractive centre, will enable you to see exactly why. It features an idyllic, winding riverside descent down to the mill, with an optional extension across meadows to the weir, and returns by way of the delightful Brakey Wood.

> **Distance** 3 miles, including the extension.
> **Terrain** Pavement, marked footpaths, quiet minor road.
> **Refreshments** The historic and characterful Swan Inn, in the centre of the village, has a restaurant and extensive gardens.
>
> **MAP**   OS Explorer 230
> **GR**   TM180772
> **PC**   IP21 5AS

START

Village green in the centre of Hoxne *(1), just up from the Swan Inn and Post Office/stores. From the green, head uphill away from the Swan to Church Hill, passing a row of houses and then two wooden posts. Keep going to the top of this fairly steep pedestrian lane, passing The White House and High House. At the top, with the church entrance *(2) opposite, turn right on the pavement, passing Oakley Terrace on the other side (formerly almshouses) and Church Close.

Not far beyond Church Close, turn left on the tree lined Watermill Lane. After approx 200yds, where the lane opens out at a fenced off concreted area and with views ahead, you have a choice – either to take the extension (recommended) or carry on, on Watermill Lane.

Optional Extension … One mile, approx, 20 mins there and back, to the weir. The weir itself is a very attractive spot and well worth the detour, with far reaching views across the meadows to the tower of All Saints church, Thorpe Abbots, and of Hoxne Mill. It is a particularly tranquil section of the river. From the top, keep straight ahead, through a metal gate, heading downhill on a leafy signposted FP. Follow the track round to the right, at the bottom, to a bridge and kissing gate. Through the gate, carry on along the path, with the river to your left, winding its way around to the weir, with its bridge and viewpoint. Retrace your steps back to the top, the same way.

Hoxne Mill

Back at the concreted area, turn left at a No Through Road sign, onto Watermill Lane. Follow this single track lane as it winds downhill, before long affording beautiful views of the river and valley to your left. As you approach the mill *(3) with its various buildings, chimney and handsome, shuttered mill house, you will see a FP sign to your right.

Take this path, up past a pink washed house on your left, then bearing left on a concrete path past old outbuildings. After passing a large wooden barn on your left, turn right at a footpath sign, passing a large modern house on your left. Turn right on a minor road between trees, away from the house. Carry on past Albion House on your left, and when you reach a road, turn right past Havensfield Happy Hens.

At the junction by Dairy Farm, turn left and follow the road round for 100 yds, then turning right at Wittons Lane. Head downhill here, and after another 400 yds or so you will come to a layby and the entrance to Brakey Wood *(4). Go through the gate and then straight ahead past an information board about the wood, soon curving round to the left on a broad, grassy path with trees to both sides. Before long you will see a stream to your RHS also.

When you come to a wooden gate leading out of the woods, cross a concrete path and keep straight ahead along the RH edge of a large field and passing the Anglian Water treatment plant. After 100 yds or so, turn right at a FP sign along the other side of the plant, soon with woods to your right again and then the gardens of a detached house. When you come to a gravelled track, just beyond the house, turn right at a FP sign, passing between conifers and then a fence to your right and a wooden house/barn to your left. Soon you will come to a fork – turn right here, and then left over a footbridge.

Follow this path as it rises and turns, with woods to your right and livestock enclosures to your left. Ignore a gate/path to your right and keep ahead alongside paddocks. Follow this gravel track straight ahead past cottages and gardens until you come out onto the road at the Hoxne Swan and village centre.

NOTES

1. For a village of about 900 people, Hoxne is an extraordinary treasure trove of history and pre-history. A short walk beyond The Swan, next to the village hall, is Goldbrook Bridge. Legend has it this is the site of the martyrdom of King Edmund in AD 870, by Danish soldiers. A small, weathered stone memorial marks the spot. A little further down the same road, in the middle of a field, is St Edmund's monument.

    No less extraordinary, in 1992, in a field near Home Farm, a metal detectorist discovered the greatest collection of C4th and C5th coins found anywhere in the Roman Empire – the Hoxne Hoard – along with many other artefacts, all now in the British Museum. The church also has displays of finds from the nearby old brick and pipe works, from various periods back to the prehistoric, with flint tools from the renowned Hoxnian Interglacial Lake.

2. The church of St Peter and St Paul is well worth a visit, not least for its series of medieval wall paintings, dating to 1390 –1400. Inside the church are informative displays and leaflets relating to the remarkable wealth of history and archaelogy in and around Hoxne.

3. Hoxne Mill. There have been mills here

HOXNE TREASURES 25

going back to the Domesday Book. The present one was built in 1846 to replace an earlier one of 1749. The chimney and engine house are evidence of the later addition of steam. (See Hoxne Heritage Group and Norfolk Mills websites)

4. Brakey Wood was one of 200 woods created nationwide to celebrate the Millenium. The 16 acre site was acquired by the Woodland Trust in 1998. It features a carving of prehistoric "Hoxne Man" as well as some unusual trees, including Black Poplar and Sequoia.

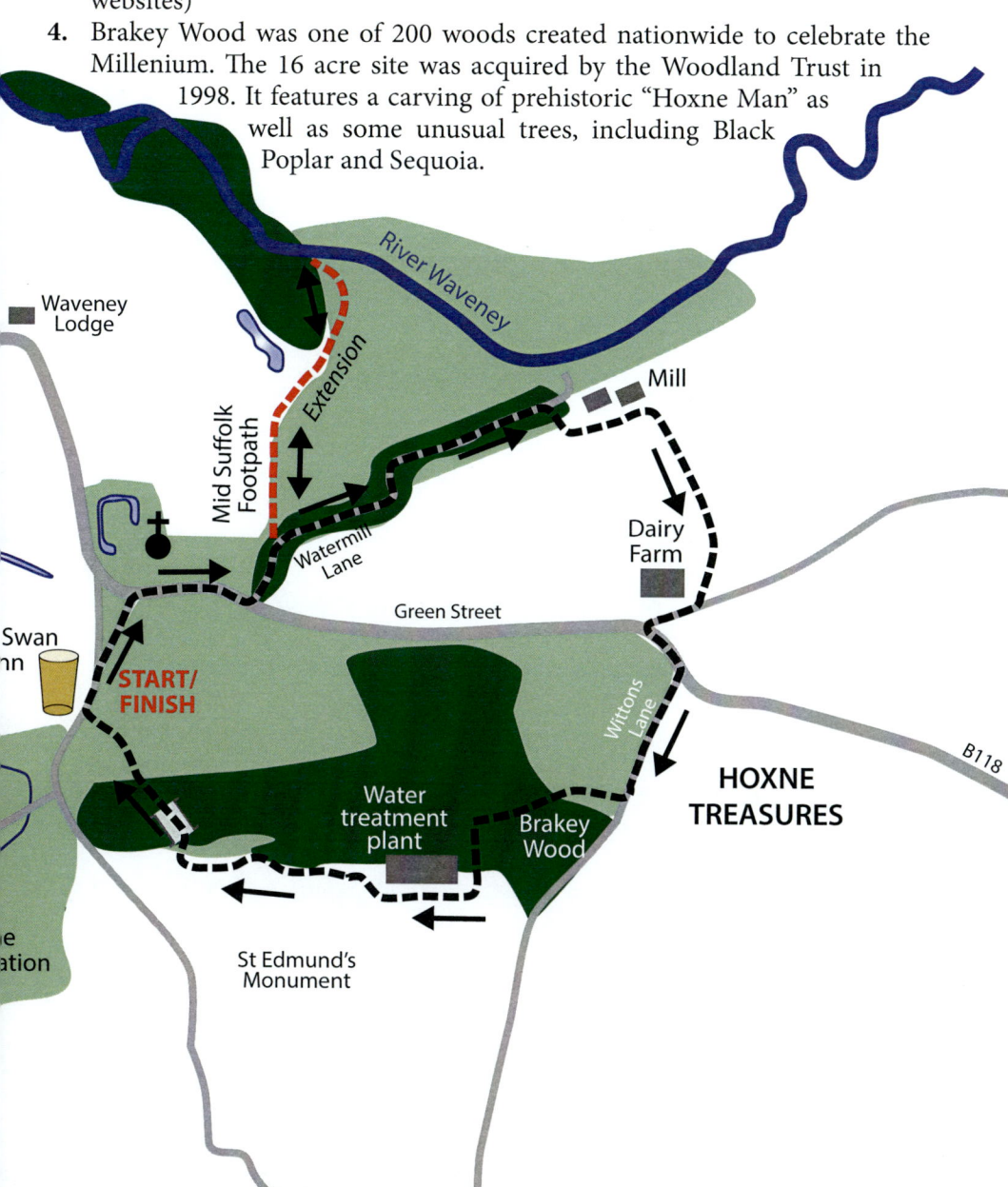

6. Syleham, Brockdish and the Angles Way

A most rewarding walk through some pleasingly hilly terrain, and with plenty of interest along the way. It takes in the two very appealing and historic villages of Syleham and Brockdish as well as a verdant and secluded riverside stretch of the Angles Way.

Distance 2 miles.
Terrain Public footpaths, including section of Angles Way; minor roads (very little traffic); pavement.
Refreshments The Old Kings Head, Brockdish. A very agreeable and atmospheric village pub. Spacious restaurant, specialising in gourmet pizzas, Italian food and tasteful jazz. Good range of local beers. Outside seating areas; occasional live music.

MAP   OS Explorer 230
GR   TM213791
PC   IP21 4LQ

START

On Syleham Rd, which runs from Brockdish to Syleham, you can park in the layby on RHS just before the bridge/weir at Syleham *(1). Cross over the bridge and turn left at the junction by a row of mill cottages, and passing by the imposing Syleham House. Stay on this minor road for a little over ½ mile, passing Waveney Terrace and heading uphill. Ignore a turning to the right (Syleham, Wingfield, Fressingfield), and as the road curves round to the left, carry on uphill (signposted Brockdish). As you are approaching the top of this longish hill, turn off sharp left, following a FP sign opposite concrete hard standing on RHS.

This path follows a large field edge before heading down through a gap into a broad tree-lined meadow sloping down to the river valley ahead. At the bottom it curves to the left, and soon you will see wooden steps down to the right, leading to a plank bridge and stile. Cross this and turn left to join the Angles Way. (**NB** Before you do this you may want to explore the path to the right a little way – there are a couple of idyllic and secluded riverside spots here, about 100 yds along, with rustic benches. A great place to dally or picnic.)

Wingfield Castle

Otherwise, follow the broad path between trees, over another stile, with the river on your right.

After a ¼ mile or so on this path, bear slightly right towards a gate ahead. After

Syleham – bridge and weir

passing through the gate, turn right, crossing a bridge and approaching farm buildings and a bungalow. Cross the tarmac farmyard (don't worry, this is a public FP) coming out onto a minor road. Straight ahead is the entrance to the small but quiet and leafy Brockdish Common. Enter here and turn right onto a path which comes out into the village at Common Lane and Shingle House.

Here, by the village hall, it's worth taking 5/10 minutes to walk up Grove Rd, opposite, as far as the Waveney Heritage Centre (see Recommended Reading section for details), formerly the village primary school, returning the same way. The road runs alongside a stream, passing some fine houses, by a raised pavement. Back at the village hall, turn left following the Angles Way sign, on Syleham Rd now. Carry on past cowsheds to your left, returning to the starting point.

NOTES
1. A water mill existed here for nearly a thousand years. Syleham Mill, on the site of what is now the row of residential cottages, was a corn mill up until 1839. It was then converted to the manufacture of a coarse linen and cotton cloth called "drabbet". It was later, in the C20th, a clothing factory, up until 1989, when it closed down. Of the mill, only the roundhouse and trestle survive.

In the vicinity ... An interesting digression. From the mill cottages, at the start of the walk, if you go the opposite way, past the cottages, you will follow a winding minor road through the elongated village of Syleham in the beautiful valley bottom. At the crossroads (Syleham Cross) with its memorial Cross, a track leads down to St Margaret's church, in its isolated and very attractive setting, which you may want to explore. Otherwise, keep straight ahead on the road, past some more houses. Another ¼ mile or so will bring you to the ancient and highly evocative Monks Hall, set back from the road on your right. Local historian Elaine Murphy has written a fascinating and absorbing "biography" of the house's thousand year history (see **Recommended Reading**).

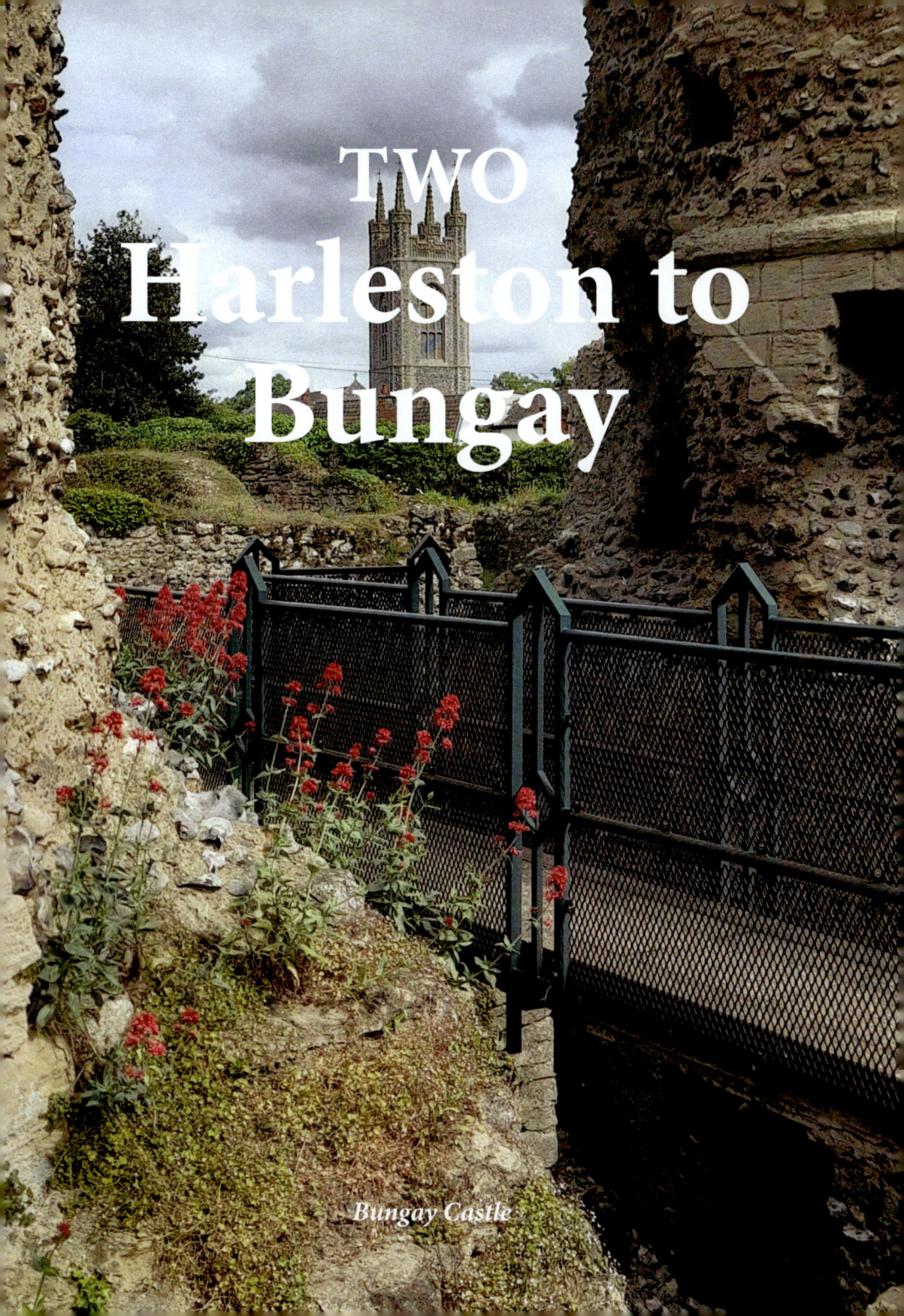

TWO
Harleston to Bungay

Bungay Castle

7. Harleston – town and country

A walk that leads from the centre of this very likeable and distinctive market town out into the more elevated surrounding countryside, with far-reaching views over the Gawdy Hall Estate and the landmark Redenhall church. The best of both worlds indeed.

> **Distance** 3 miles.
> **Terrain** Pavement through town, minor roads, cycle path and footpaths.
> **Refreshments** Harleston has an abundance of cafes, bakeries, pubs and restaurants to choose from, mostly around The Thoroughfare and Market Place.
>
> **MAP** OS Explorer 230
> **GR** TM245833
> **PC** IP20 9BW

START

The Market Place *(1) by JD Youngs Hotel. (Free parking is available nearby in the car park at the back of St Johns Church on Broad St.) Set off down the main shopping street, The Thoroughfare, passing the Clock Tower *(2) and old coaching inn the Swan Hotel. Carry on past Bullock Fair Close, then turn left into a yard after a handsome bow windowed building, presently a café and shop, at a sign for the Masonic Rooms. Follow the gravelled yard *(3) round to the right and then keep straight ahead on Eversons Lane. Turn left on Station Rd, passing to the left of the old station building *(4) and then straight on at Station Hill.

Head downhill, past the Army Cadets HQ on your right. Cross the bridge at the bottom and then bear slightly left, uphill, on a narrow lane, signposted "Starston, Pulham St Mary". Take care here as there is no verge or pavement for a short way. At the top of this hill, where the road turns left, take a right turn at 4 posts, on a cycleway/path. You will see the tower of St Mary Redenhall ahead.

Carry on down the path passing through a metal gate and then turning left at a give way sign. You will soon pass a sign for Lodge Farm and Gawdy Hall Estate *(5) further along on your left, shortly followed by another entrance and gatehouse. Carry on downhill towards a row of conifers, ignoring FP signs to left and right.

Harleston: The Thoroughfare

When you reach the conifers, turn off to your right, on a path downhill through the trees. Where the conifers end, turn right and follow a track running alongside a dyke to your RHS and through trees, eventually coming out onto a minor road, with houses and a bridge to your left. Cross the bridge over the stream (The Beck) and then immediately right by two cottages. You will shortly join the main road, where you need to turn right ("Harleston 1"), walking on the footpath.

After approx. 250 yards, at the "Welcome to Harleston" sign, cross over and follow a FP sign uphill into a field. There are fine views from the top, back over to

Gawdy Hall Estate. Stay on this path across a grassy meadow, towards and then alongside bungalows. When you come out onto a road, turn right, signposted "town centre".

Carry straight on, past Lovat Close and the Catholic chapel. At a junction by a post box, keep straight ahead till you come to a No Through Road sign, at Straight Lane. Carry on down this pedestrian thoroughfare. The path soon narrows and then emerges by the war memorial and Victorian church of St John, where you will keep straight ahead to return to the Market Place.

NOTES

1. (Not to be confused with the nearby Old Market Place). There has been a weekly market here since 1259, when the right to hold a "fair" was first granted. The street pattern of the historic centre also dates back to the C13th. For a small town, Harleston has an exceptional concentration and range of historic buildings, 163 being listed, from the medieval period onwards. Market day is Wednesday.
2. The Italianate clock tower is a landmark in the town (and its tallest building) and a familiar sound as it chimes the hours. It was built in 1873 on the site of the former, medieval parish church and chapel of ease of St John, demolished in the same year.
3. These yards are very much a feature of the Harleston townscape, and date back to medieval times. Each was associated with a particular trade or small industry – wheel wrights, tinsmiths, saddlers, gunsmiths, weavers and basketmakers, for example – and the buildings fronting the street became their shops.
4. The station was on the old Waveney Valley branch line, which closed to passengers in 1953. It ran from Tivetshall in Norfolk to Beccles in Suffolk.
5. Gawdy Hall itself was demolished in 1939. It was originally built in the 1500s. The Gawdys were a family of lawyers who flourished in Norfolk and Suffolk in the C16th and C17th. Elizabeth I is thought to have stayed here in 1578. The 1,500 acre estate was up for sale (March 2022) for a guide price of £24m.

HARLESTON – TOWN AND COUNTRY 33

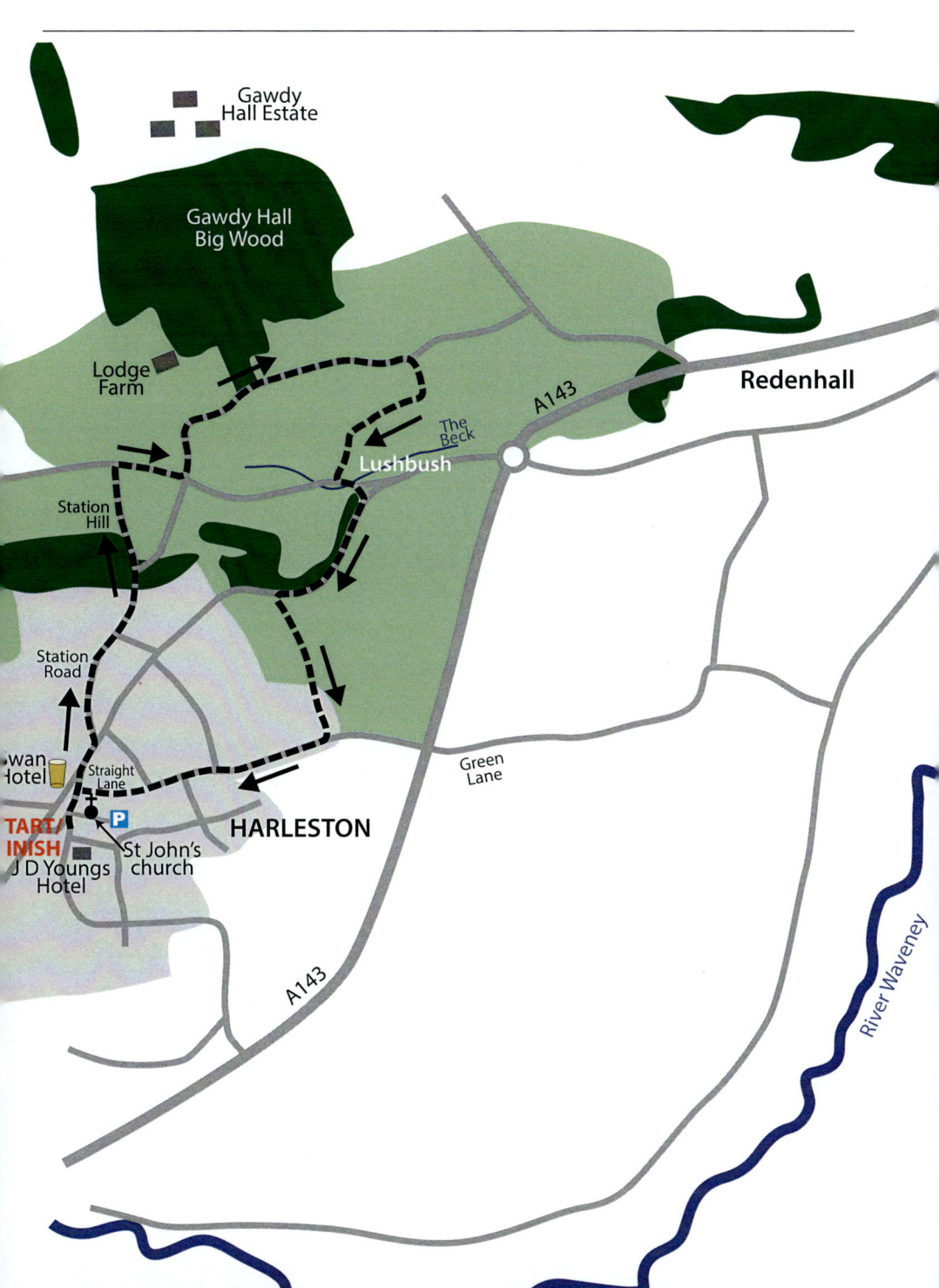

34 HARLESTON TO BUNGAY

8. Redenhall and Wortwell

A fairly short but very satisfying route with lofty and far-reaching views over the Waveney Valley and surrounding countryside. Starts in the churchyard of St Mary's Redenhall before descending into the valley bottom at Mendham marshes and Wortwell village.

Distance 2½ miles (including short detour to memorial)..
Terrain Footpaths, minor road, pavement. NB Valley bottom is liable to flooding in winter.
Refreshments The Wortwell Bell is a friendly local in the centre of the village, with a restaurant and pleasant outdoor seating area.

MAP   OS Explorer 230
GR   TM263843
PC   IP20 9QW

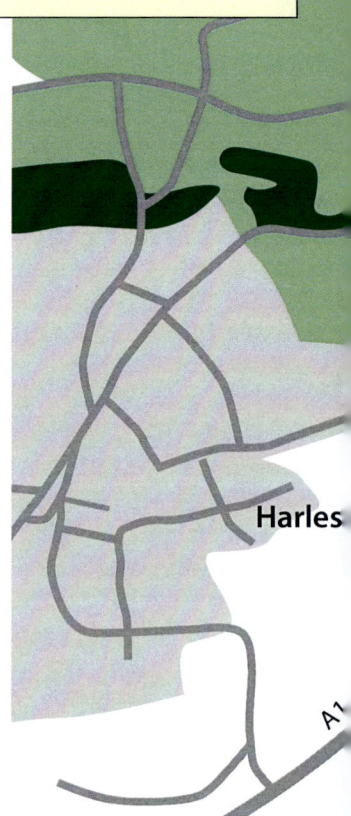

START
St Mary's church, Redenhall *(1), about a mile outside of Harleston, off the A143 at the roundabout and in the hamlet of Redenhall. Take the signposted FP through a gate into the churchyard, walking at right angles to the road, and passing in front of the magnificent Perpendicular tower and under a yew tree. Carry straight on towards another gate at the end of the churchyard and into a field. Keep straight ahead, with a hedge to your left.

When you reach a minor road (Cooks Lane) turn right. After about 200 yards, turn sharp left on Cuckoo Lane. *(2) At this point you have extensive and uninterrupted views ahead, over this central part of the Waveney Valley. Soon you will be heading down a steep hill to the valley bottom, with trees on both sides as you descend.

At the bottom of the hill, turn left on Low Rd, with the wide expanse of Mendham Marshes stretching away to your right. Carry on past Low Tree Farm, soon

REDENHALL AND WORTWELL 35

with more houses on your left, and now on the outskirts of Wortwell village. Just after No. 88, take a signposted FP ("Circular walk") to your left and uphill between hedges. Bear left at the top and follow the twists and turns of this path across a field edge. You will see two roads ahead – the A143 in the distance, and before it a minor road. When you reach the minor road, at Wortwell Old School house, turn left onto it, crossing over and following the pavement back towards the landmark church tower and starting point.

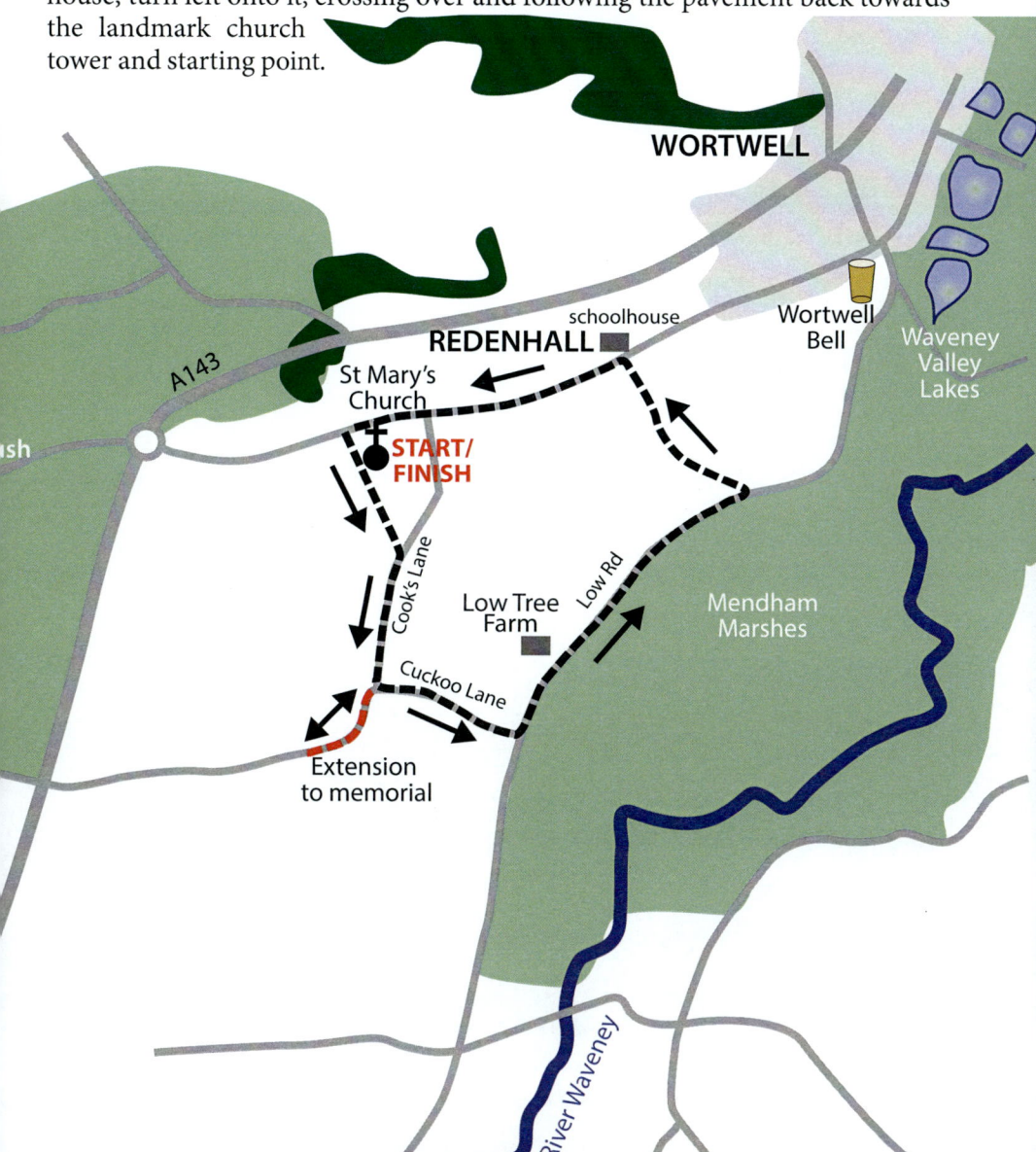

NOTES

1. St Mary's church, or the Assumption of the Blessed Virgin Mary, to give it its full title, is a grade 1 listed building and a much loved landmark in this part of the Waveney Valley. The splendid tower, nearly 60 ft tall and already situated on a hill, was started in 1460 and completed in 1514. The views from the top, if you are lucky enough to be there on an open day, are magnificent.

2. If you carry straight on here for another 200 yards or so, before descending on Cuckoo Lane, you will come to the very poignant memorial to the 22 US servicemen who were killed in a mid air crash on this spot in April 1945, not long before the end of the war. They were returning to nearby Flixton airbase after a mission over Regensburg, Bavaria. There were no survivors.

Redenhall, St Mary – view from tower

9. Withersdale Street

Belying the popular notion that Norfolk is flat, this bracing walk begins with a steep ascent affording really impressive and unspoilt views. Dropping down into a very attractive wooded vale, the route circles back via a bridleway to the starting point close to Mendham Priory.

Distance 3 miles.
Terrain Footpaths, bridleway, minor roads (very little traffic).
Refreshments Harleston (approx. 2 miles) has an excellent range of cafes, pubs, eateries and amenities. The Sir Alfred Munnings is a beautifully situated small hotel and pub in the nearby village of Mendham. The distinguished artist Munnings was born in the village, at the Mill on the Waveney here – itself well worth a visit.

MAP   OS Explorer 230
GR   TM262810
PC   IP20 0JH

START

The aptly named Withersdale Street is a linear village running along the B1123 Harleston to Metfield road. Just after the village sign, when you are coming from Harleston, turn right on a bend at a turnoff signed Fressingfield and Weybread. A hundred yards or so along this road, at a metal fence on your left, climb over a gate/stile into a hilly field. Here you are more or less opposite the entrance to the grand hilltop house Mendham Priory *(1) Head uphill, following a fence and the edge of a wood (Bluebell Wood) round to your right. The view is quite something, and the closer you get to the top, the better it becomes.

Stay alongside the fence and trees, soon dipping down into a new vale. You will shortly turn slightly back on yourself to head down towards the road by way of a wooden gate, which you may need to climb over. Turn left on the road, and at the first big tree on your RHS, take the marked FP to the right (hedge may be slightly overgrown). Carry on and cross a wooden bridge. Turn left soon after the bridge on a path into and through woods. Keep straight ahead when this becomes a broad track. When you come out onto a road, turn left, and shortly afterwards turn right at the junction (signposted Cratfield and Laxfield).

Stay on this winding, wooded lane as it heads gradually uphill, ignoring a

Bridleway sign to your left and passing Coverts Chase. After approx. ½ mile when you reach a three way junction, turn left (signposted Withersdale 1). After approx. a third of a mile on this road you will come to a Bridleway sign on your LHS. Follow this, across the middle of a large field, towards a line of bushes ahead.

When you reach these, keep straight ahead on the Bridleway, soon with bushes to both sides. Stay on this path till you arrive back at the Bridleway sign you passed earlier, near Coverts Chase, then turn right, heading for the 3 way signpost. Keep straight ahead on the minor road here, through the vale and back to the starting point, near Mendham Priory – approx. ½ mile.

NOTES

1. Mendham Priory was sold in 2021 for £2.4m. It is a grand C19th house standing in 27 acres of parkland. It has its own 7 ¼" railway, complete with sidings, which runs around the periphery of the parkland. It is named after the C12th Cluniac Priory, of which virtually nothing remains, on nearby Mendham Marshes. Some of the stones from the original were used in the construction

Withersdale Street, North view

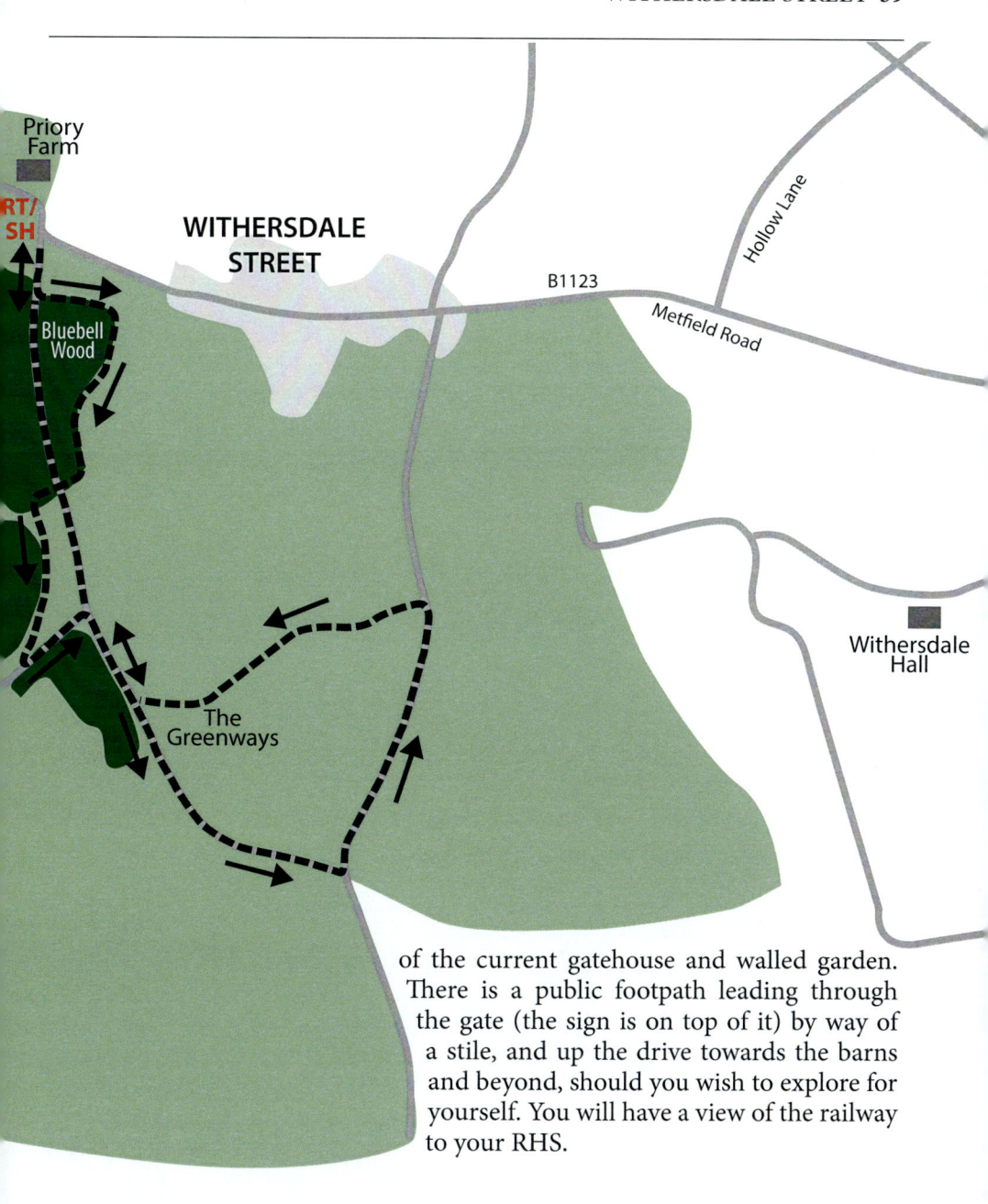

WITHERSDALE STREET **39**

Priory Farm
RT/SH
Bluebell Wood
WITHERSDALE STREET
Hollow Lane
B1123
Metfield Road
The Greenways
Withersdale Hall

of the current gatehouse and walled garden. There is a public footpath leading through the gate (the sign is on top of it) by way of a stile, and up the drive towards the barns and beyond, should you wish to explore for yourself. You will have a view of the railway to your RHS.

10. *Wortwell Mill and Limbourne Common*

A very satisfying and varied walk whose attractions include the historic riverside mill buildings and hall, two bridges over the Waveney, far reaching valley views, a lovely wooded section of the Angles Way and two village pubs.

Distance 3 miles.
Terrain Track, footpaths inc. section of Angles Way, pavement, minor roads. Waterproof footwear is essential – Limbourne Common especially, is very low lying.
Refreshments The Wortwell Bell; The Black Swan, Homersfield. Both are pleasant village pubs with gardens and restaurants. The Black Swan is particularly spacious and well situated, with camping and caravanning site adjoining. Pura Vida plant centre, which you pass on your way into Wortwell, has a speciality coffee shop and café, with indoor and outdoor seating. On the opposite side of the A143 is The Dove restaurant and coffee shop.

MAP   OS Explorer 230
GR   TM276848
PC   IP20 0HH

START

Layby next to The Wortwell Bell pub, in the centre of Wortwell village. From The Bell, take Low Rd, signposted Mendham. After about 100 yards bear left on a private road, with a sign for Wortwell Hall and Mill. In approx. ½ mile you will reach the very attractive Wortwell Hall, set back on LHS. Follow the road round, with a pond on your left, to a bridge leading to the mill. Cross over, and pass in front of the mill *(1) to another bridge, wooden this time. Cross this, to a wooden gate and causeway, with stile.

Once over the stile, keep straight ahead in line with the footbridge across a field, towards a white house. You are now on Limbourne

Wortwell Mill

WORTWELL MILL AND LIMBOURNE COMMON 41

Common. The path then bends around to another stile. Cross this and keep straight ahead towards a line of trees. Cross over another stile, with Angles Way sign, into woods, and with a stream on your left. Follow this wooded path, with a steep bank on RHS, for about ¾ mile until it comes out onto a minor road.

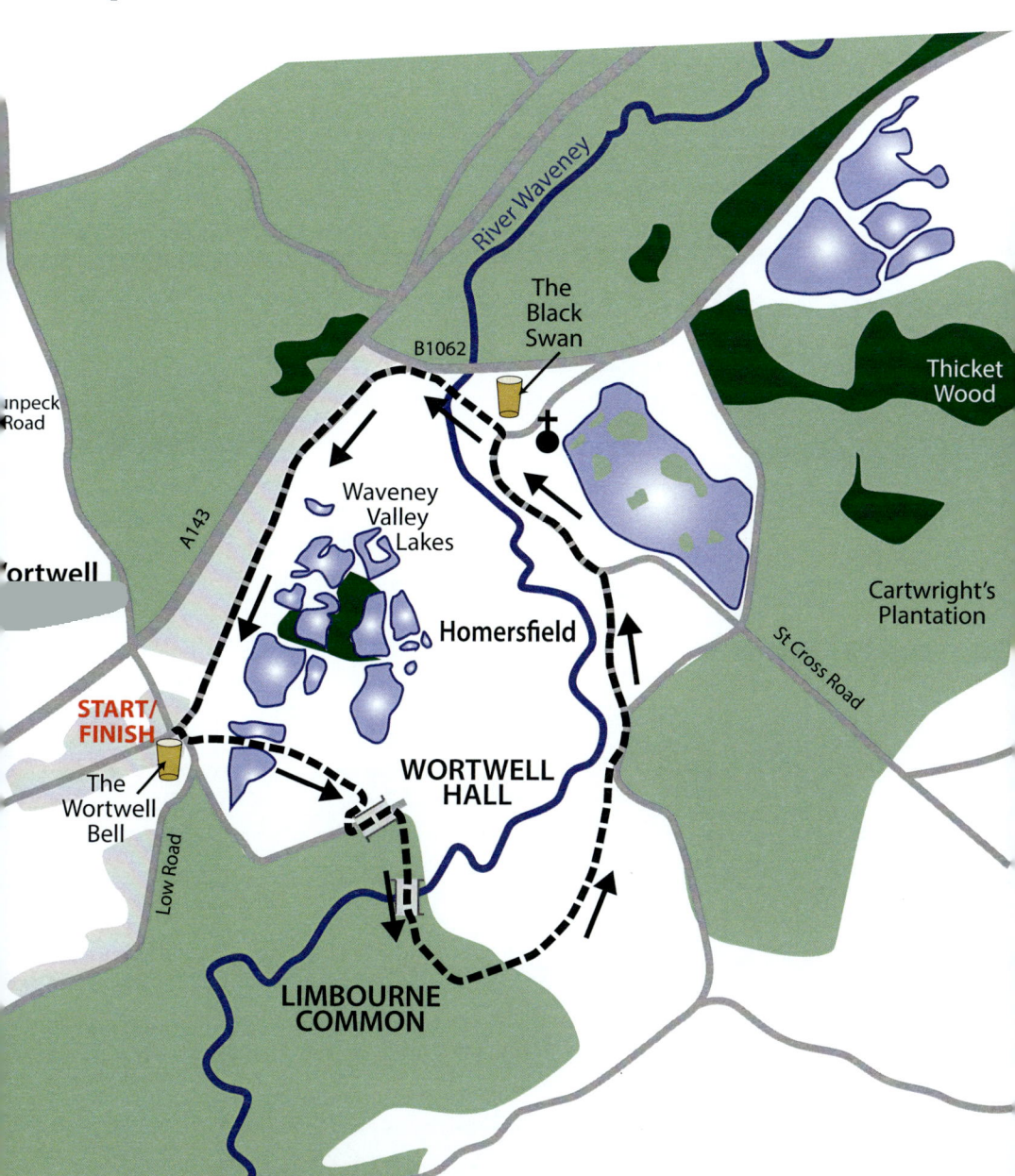

Flixton Air Museum

Turn left here, heading towards a house and farm buildings. Turn left again just before the buildings, following the "Otter Vale Walks" sign. At the next road junction turn left, signposted "Homersfield ¼ ". Follow this minor road into the village, with the marshes away to your left, and a steep wooded bank to your right, with the tower of St Mary's Homersfield visible above.

When you reach the green and playground, turn left, soon passing The Black Swan *(2) on your right. Keep straight ahead, crossing the concrete bridge over the Waveney *(3). Walk through the small riverside recreation area and carpark, and turn left at the exit, on pavement. Turn left again at a sign for Wortwell, passing a bus shelter. Cross over the High Road here, and follow the pavement into and through the village. You will pass a sign for Waveney Valley Lakes Lodges and Goodswens Garage on your left, before arriving back at The Bell.

NOTES
1. Wortwell Mill is a very attractive, restored, grade 2 listed watermill and millhouse, dating from 1750. It is a white, weatherboarded, three storey building in a spectacular riverside setting.
2. Over the fireplace in the cosy bar of the Black Swan is an intact mammoth tusk, discovered in a nearby gravel pit (see the information board next to the nearby playground for further information.) The Homersfield area contains fairly extensive gravel deposits, formed in the Ice Age, which are still being worked. These provided grazing land for animals such as woolly mammoth and rhinoceros, bison and reindeer which would have been roaming the grasslands of the Waveney Valley 60,000 years ago.
3. Homersfield Bridge has the distinction of being the oldest concrete bridge in Great Britain. It was built in 1869 and has a single span of 50ft. The adjacent amenity area is popular, especially in summer, with canoeists, anglers, wild swimmers and picnickers.

In the vicinity ... The Norfolk and Suffolk Aviation Museum in nearby Flixton, on the B1062 from Homersfield to Bungay, is not to be missed (www.aviationmuseum.net). Run almost entirely by volunteers, and with free entry, it is a gem of a collection, with over 60 historic aircraft on display outdoors and in a number of hangars. There is also a boardwalk, the Adair Walk, leading down to the Waveney.

11. Alburgh – Holbrook Hill

A fairly steep climb at the outset is soon rewarded with fine valley views to the South, and likewise at the end of the walk, from a different vantage point. A bracing and enjoyable walk, anything but flat, through woods and farmland around the outskirts of the village of Alburgh.

Distance 3 miles.
Terrain Footpaths, bridleway, minor roads. Paths can get quite boggy.
Refreshments The recently reopened Dove Restaurant and coffee shop is adjacent to the starting point of the walk. On the opposite side of the A143, at the junction, Pura Vida plant centre has a café with attractive indoor and outdoor seating areas.
The Bell in Wortwell is an agreeable village pub and restaurant. Alburgh is also home to the excellent Grain Brewery (South Farm, Tunbeck Rd).

MAP OS Explorer 230
GR TM281859
PC IP20 OEP

START

On the A143 Harleston to Bungay road, turn off left at crossroads near Wortwell, following road sign "Alburgh 1 ¼". At the junction of Denton Low Rd and Station Rd, near The Dove restaurant, head uphill on Station Rd. Towards the top of the hill, at a muddy layby, turn off left at a stile and wooden fence. Over the stile, walk alongside the fence and then hedge, at the top edge of a grassy field, with fine views to your left over a tree lined meandering stream and beyond.

After roughly 300 yds you will start to drop down into a vale, with a metal gate at the bottom. Turn immediately right, after the gate, heading uphill to another one. Keep straight ahead here, alongside the hedge, to the top. Turn right at the top and carry on along the

Lizards, Homersfield

Holbrook Hill, Alburgh

edge of another field, with fence on your left. Keep straight ahead at the next gate to another double gate, where you will rejoin the road you started on, but further up.

Turn left onto the road, soon passing Holbrook Hall on your right. This road winds round into the village of Alburgh. About 100 yds beyond the half-timbered Chestnut Cottage, and just before two bungalows on your left, take a FP off to the right, between trees (not marked and rather narrow, so don't miss it!).

Before long this path opens out, along the edge of a field to your right. Keep straight ahead until you meet a muddy track at right angles. Turn right here, following the track, and soon bearing slightly right to follow a path between trees ahead. After about 400 yds you will come to a junction of paths at a Public Bridleway sign. Carry straight on here, with the hedge to your right, towards farm buildings and with views of open country to your left.

When you reach the farm buildings and farmhouse, the path becomes a cinder track, shortly joining a road. Turn right here, soon heading downhill past an imposing house at the end of a long avenue of trees, to your left. At the bottom of the road (Round House Hill – you'll soon

ALBURGH – HOLBROOK HILL   45

see why) turn right at the junction. Follow this road, on the final stretch back to the starting point, passing Station Rd Motors.

In the vicinity … You may be interested to visit the remains of a motte and bailey castle in Yarrow Wood, a mile or so north of the village near the evocatively named Hangman's Hill and (presumably related) Misery Corner! The castle and moat remains, on what was an earlier pagan site, are now a Scheduled Ancient Monument and in the care of the National Trust. Although there is not a lot left of the castle, it is an atmospheric site in a pretty remote location. There is an information board near the entrance.

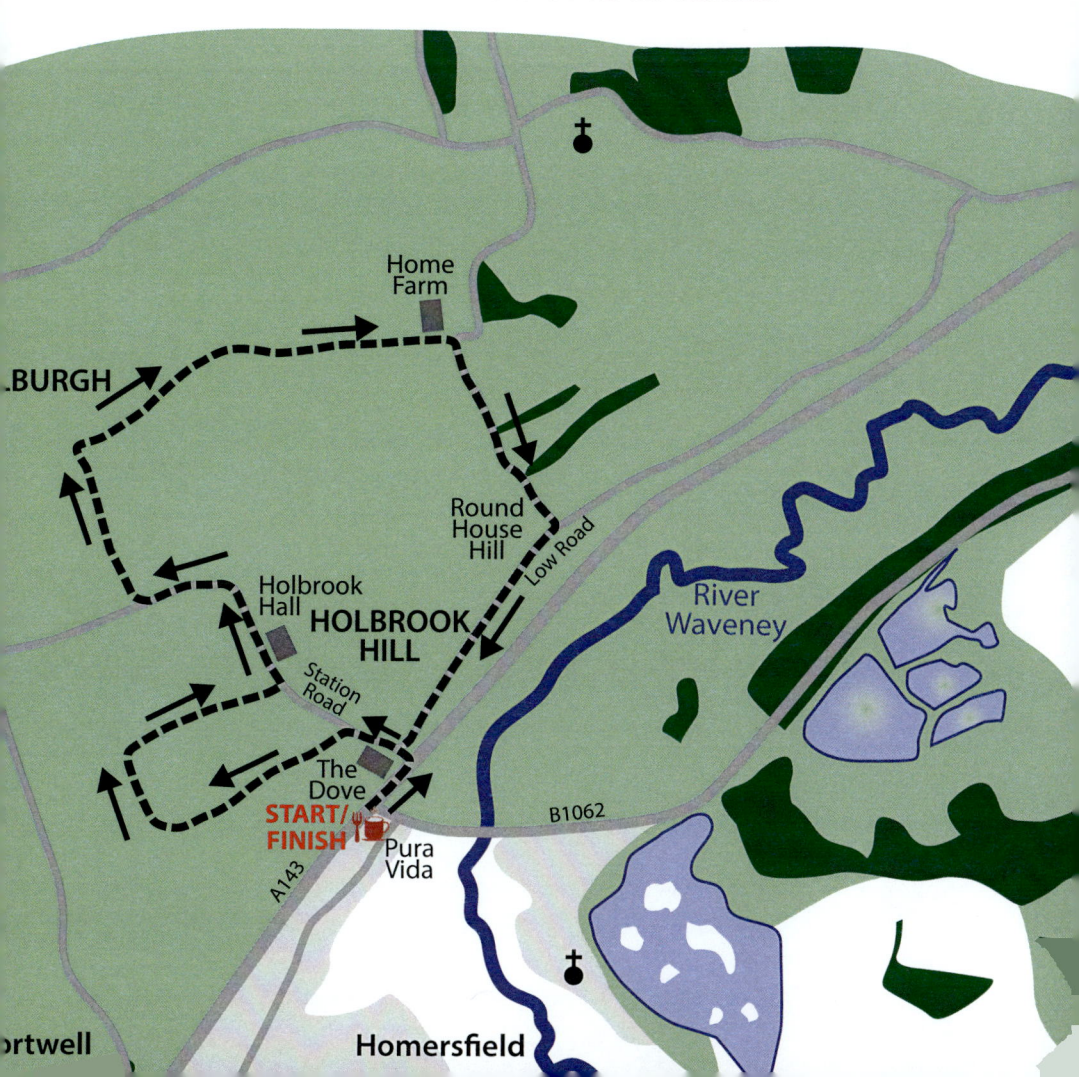

12. *St Peter, South Elmham*

At the heart of the fascinating and remote-seeming area of North Suffolk known as The Saints, this delightful short walk takes in the church itself, the hamlet and surrounding countryside as well as the moated medieval hall of St Peter's with its brewery, shop and restaurant.

Distance 2½ miles.
Terrain Marked footpaths, minor roads and track.
Refreshments St Peter's Hall. Trio's Restaurant is currently open Thursday – Sat. 10-5; Friday eves from 7-11pm for tapas and live music; Sat. Supper Club 1st and 3rd Saturdays.
Tel 01986 782288 for info.

MAP OS Explorer 231
GR TM335847
PC NR35 1NG

START

The church of St Peter, South Elmham, within the wider area of "The Saints" *(1) two or three miles to the south of Bungay. Coming out of the churchyard, turn right uphill and then shortly afterwards left at a junction by a postbox and bench (signposted Flixton and Homersfield). Keep straight ahead, on a tree-lined road, past Willow Dykes Barn and Cottage, with views of open country away to your left. At a junction, turn left (signposted All Saints and St Margaret), winding downhill alongside hedges. At a FP sign, just before a white bridge, turn left across a field, heading towards and shortly passing through a gap in the hedge/trees.

Keep straight ahead, with the church tower soon visible ahead, and ignoring a FP to the right which crosses over a wooden bridge. At the end of this field, the path narrows, with a hedge to the left, and a fenced paddock to the right, followed by another. Where this broad, grassy path comes out onto a road, turn left and head uphill back to the church.

Keep on past the church, but this time bear right at the junction, following a sign for St Peter's Brewery. After approx. 200 yards, you will come to the entrance drive to St Peter's Hall and Brewery *(2). Carry on past this for another 150 yards, and just beyond a lay-by, turn left at a FP sign. Follow this path, with hedge to your left and large field to right for about 200 yards. As you approach the Hall, you will see the moat to your LHS. Where this ends, turn left through a grassy gap towards the brewery shop and buildings. After exploring the Hall and grounds/facilities return to the church by the main approach road.

St Peter's Hall

NOTES

1. "The Saints" is the collective name given to a group of scattered villages, and in some cases tiny hamlets, in this part of North Suffolk, each with its own patron saint and, in most cases, church. There are eight in all, with another four "Ilketshall Saints" (see separate walk) slightly further to the West. The area feels both sparsely populated and decidedly untroubled by the modern world. It is an altogether fascinating and unique area to explore at leisure, for example by bicycle, although there is always a good chance of finding yourself lost. A number of the Saints villages are ranged around sizeable commons – St Margaret, St Michael and All Saints for example. St Michael is also one of only two "thankful" villages in Suffolk i.e. those whose soldiers all returned alive after WW1. The nearby moated Benedictine priory church of St Michael's, Rumburgh, founded in about 1065, is a memorable sight and a visibly ancient and unusual one, well worth the detour.

2. St Peter's Hall is a historic, moated manor house dating from 1280. It was extended in 1539 using salvaged materials from nearby Flixton Priory at the time of the dissolution of the monasteries. The place has a striking sense of antiquity, both inside and out, perhaps accentuated by the remoteness of its location, seemingly in the middle of nowhere. The brewery was established in 1996, in former agricultural buildings adjacent to the Hall. The Hall has recently re-opened following refurbishment. Sitting at one of the tables outside, by the moat, is an experience not to be missed, especially on a sunny day.

13. *Earsham Mill and Marshes*

Just to the West of Bungay, this walk describes a large square across the marshes known as Marston Moor. It is an expansive, watery landscape and an interesting one, with paths mostly alongside or close to rivers, and featuring fine views as well as a historic mill in a very attractive setting.

Distance 2 miles.
Terrain Footpaths, track, short stretch of road (on pavement). NB Waterproof footwear essential, especially in winter months, as paths liable to be waterlogged.
Refreshments Grumpy's Café, Earsham Mill has outside seating in an idyllic location, by the mill waters; The Queen's Head, Earsham is a real ale pub and brewery, likewise with outdoor seating. Nearby Bungay also has a good selection of eateries, in the vicinity of Earsham St and the Butter Cross. The Green Dragon pub and Brewery (est. 1991) on Broad St is a unique local institution, relaxed and bohemian. It has a sizeable covered yard, occasionally with live music.

MAP OS Explorer OL 40
GR TM326888
PC NR35 2TQ

START
All Saints church, Earsham *(1) From the road in front of the church, take your time to explore the adjacent complex of mill buildings and businesses, where there is ample parking *(2). Coming back out of the yard, take the unmade up track signposted "Marston Moor". Go past a row of six terraced houses towards an arched bridge, of brick.

Here it is well worth taking a slight detour to explore the recently restored crossing over the Waveney. Just after the cottages and before the arched bridge, turn right on a narrow, fenced path, with a canalised waterway to your left. At the end of this path you will arrive at the first of three new metal and timber bridges, with attractive views over to the old mill buildings and mill race. The third bridge crosses the Waveney itself, with views across farmland (Stow Fen) to distant hills.

50 HARLESTON TO BUNGAY

Retrace your steps to the arched bridge and six cottages, turning right over the bridge, and soon passing wooden bungalows and a Scout HQ on your right. This rough track gradually becomes a narrower path, and crosses the river via a wooden bridge. Once over, turn immediate left, with the river to your LHS, and pasture and hills away to the right.

After approx. ¾ mile, the path climbs up onto the road at a fence/gate and bridge, just outside of Bungay now. Turn left and follow this road, on the pavement, back towards Earsham. At a wooden gate, just after the next, white bridge, take a FP to your left, back across the moor, with a stream to your left now. This will eventually bring you back full circle (or square, more accurately) to the bridge and six cottages followed by the church. You will see the church spire ahead as you retrace your steps to the start.

NOTES

1. Grade 1 listed All Saints is unusual for Norfolk and Suffolk in having a pointed spire, probably added to the C14th tower in around 1700. For a fairly small village, it is a church on a decidedly grand scale. It has a gallery, for musicians, and an abundance of vibrant and colourful stained glass.
2. Earsham Mill is a brick built watermill dating back to 1862, although there has been a mill here for a thousand years, since Saxon times. It was sold in 2019, and is now (2022) undergoing restoration. The site is a fascinating and developing one and is home to a diverse range of businesses

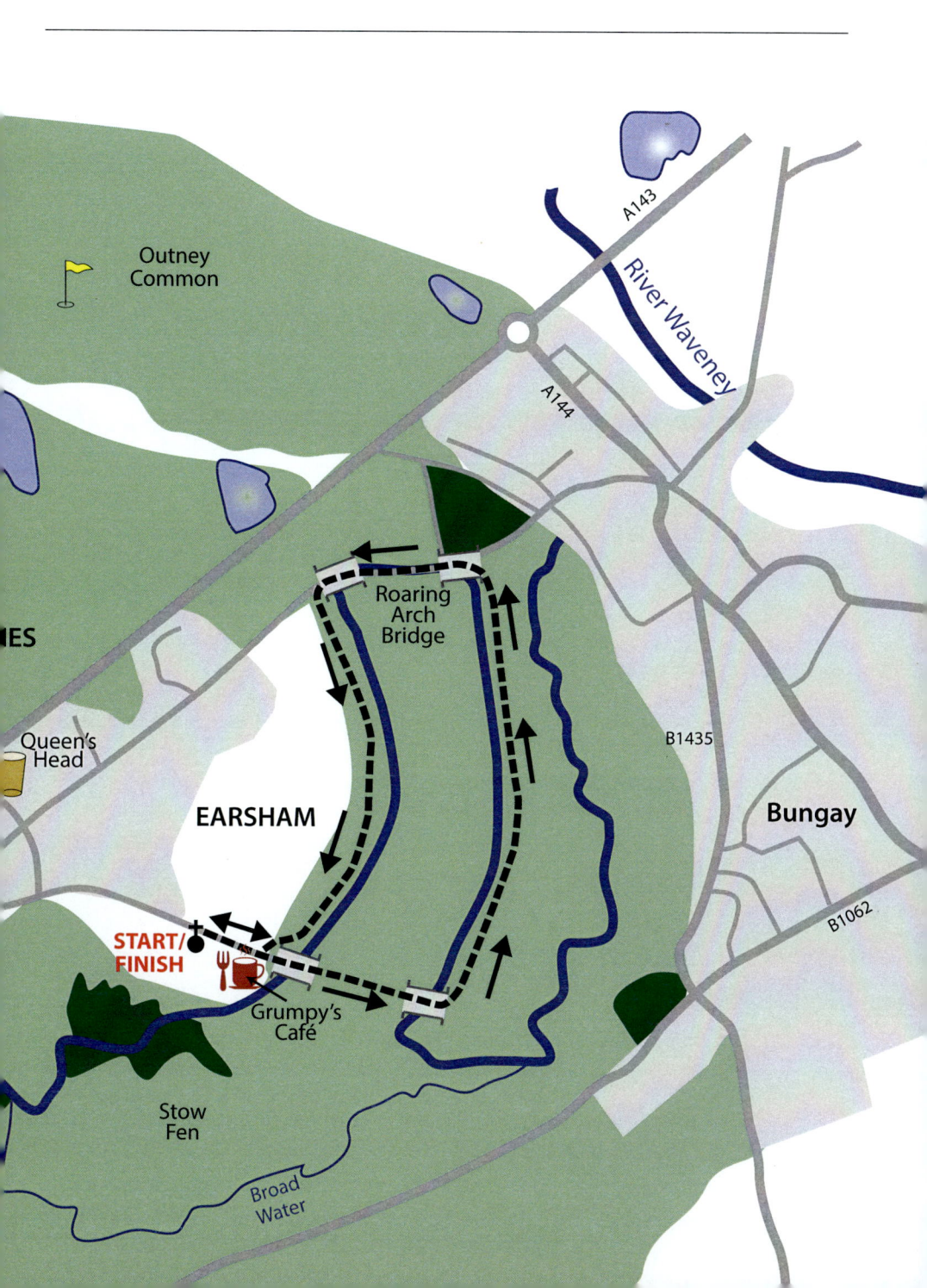

EARSHAM MILL AND MARSHES **51**

Earsham Mill

from truck repair, scaffolding and sheds to pet supplies, an art gallery, speciality coffee shop and gym.

In the vicinity ... Bungay is enclosed by a great defensive loop of the Waveney and is an ancient town that is easily (and best) explored on foot. There was a Great Fire here in 1688 which badly damaged 400 buildings. The domed Butter Cross in the centre was built the following year to commemorate this, along with many fine new Georgian houses, such as those in Earsham St, with its vibrant independent shops and eating places. In a town of only 5,000 people, there are nearly 200 listed buildings. C12th Bigod's Castle, the churches of St Mary and Holy Trinity, with its Saxon tower, and the nearby remains of the Benedictine Priory are all Grade 1 designated – i.e. "of exceptional interest".

Entrance to Bigod's Castle is through the adjacent Jesters Café, which has a pleasant outdoor seating area. Nearby Castle Hills boardwalk, when open, affords excellent views of Outney Common, Bath Hills and beyond. A walk down Bridge St to the river and alongside it through Falcon Meadows (now saved for posterity, thankfully) to the old mill buildings by way of the second bridge is also highly recommended. For entertainment, the historic Fisher Theatre is another gem, with an interesting story of its own.

THREE
Bungay to Beccles

Broome Lake

14. Wainford Maltings

Wainford Maltings is a fascinating confluence of waterways and collection of historic buildings. This very enjoyable circuit takes you up into the village of Mettingham, with fine and far reaching views back across the Waveney floodplain, returning along the valley bottom.

> **Distance** 3 miles.
> **Terrain** Footpaths, including a section of the Angles Way; bridleway; minor roads, some without pavement.
> **Refreshments** Nearby Bungay has an excellent selection of cafes, pubs and eateries, in and around the historic centre.
>
> **MAP** OS Explorer OL 40
> **GR** TM350901
> **PC** NR35 ITA

START
Lay-by just before the bridge, and landmark silo at Wainford Sluice. Cross over the bridge, heading South past the Silo *(1), Wainford Mill House *(2) and the Old Grain Store. Carry on over a second, hump back bridge on Wainford Rd. Take care on this stretch as there is no footway. When you reach a road junction ahead, take the 2nd left on the B1062, soon passing the Mettingham village sign. Cross over the road and walk uphill on the grass verge till you come, shortly, to a bridleway sign pointing to the right. This path takes you uphill across two large fields, with distant views behind.

When you come out at a road, follow the Angles Way sign straight ahead, past two bungalows (20 Vicarage Lane). The road soon turns to the right but instead turn off on the Angles Way FP, following the sign. After approx. 200 yards, turn left on a minor road (Rectory Lane).

Broome

Bungay

B1435

WAINFORD MALTINGS 55

Carry on down Rectory Lane, passing houses and then the village hall, with views of the church tower ahead (All Saints Mettingham). At the junction with the B1062, by the Tally Ho Antiques car park, turn right. Just past the antiques centre, but before you get to the churchyard entrance, cross over the B1062 and take a track ahead. After approx. 50 yds, turn right in front of the Anglia Water facility, alongside a metal fence.

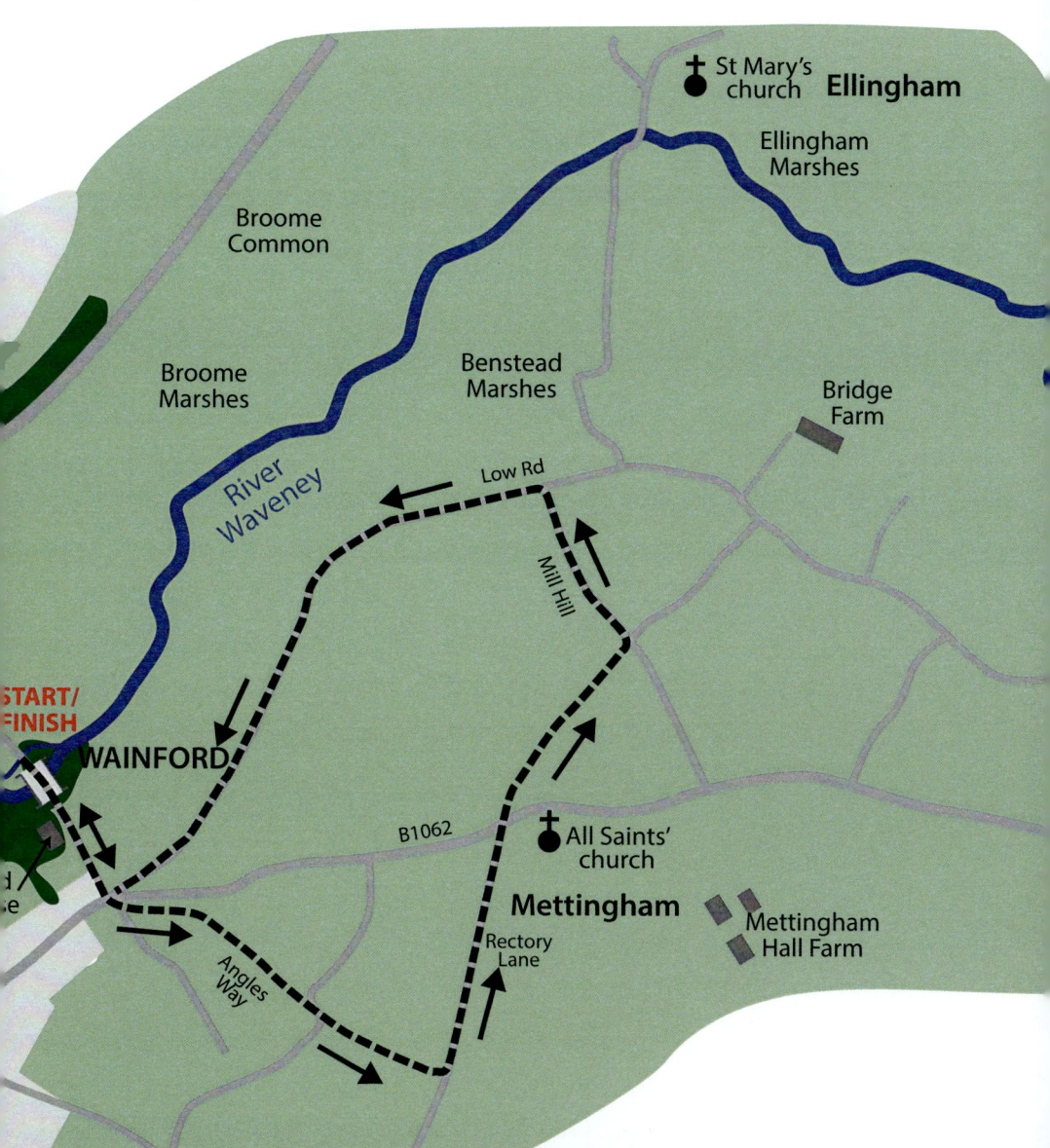

Wainford Silo

Follow this tree-lined path for approx. a third of a mile till you come to a junction of minor roads, at a gate. Turn left here on Mill Hill and carry on for approx. ½ mile, going first uphill, past houses, and then downhill again. When you come to another junction, turn left on Low Rd, signposted "Bungay 2".

Stay on this quiet minor road for approx. 1 mile, along the valley bottom, soon passing the curious Coach House and Valley Tower on your right. When you reach the junction with Wainford Rd, turn right and retrace your steps to the mill and starting point, re-crossing the two bridges.

NOTES
1. The Silo was originally built in 1958 as a grain silo, and was decommissioned in 2016. Much of it is unsafe for public use. However, it is now starting to be repurposed as an events space, with incredible views, including large scale dining events (July 2021). http://www.wainford.co.uk/thesilo
2. The double fronted Georgian mill house was renovated c. 2008 by two local brothers, and is available to rent as a self catering property. There has been a mill here since at least 1444, but the current buildings date back to the mid 1800s. Until the 1960s they were still in use as a mill and maltings, before falling into disrepair. Wainford was an important military station during the Roman occupation of Britain, and the favoured crossing point over the River Waveney at that time. It is popular with canoeists and anglers.

15. Mettingham Castle

Leading to, and around, the atmospheric C14th castle, with its remaining gatehouse and walls, this figure of eight walk explores the historic village of Mettingham and environs, and includes a section of the Angles Way, a shady, wooded bridleway.

> **Distance** 2½ miles, with visit to church.
> **Terrain** Bridleway and footpaths, including section of Angles Way; minor roads; grass verge.
> **Refreshments** The Tally Ho used to be a pub and then a tearoom in a former life. Luckily however, nearby Bungay has an excellent range of eateries, particularly in the vicinity of Earsham Street.
>
> MAP   OS Explorer OL 40
> GR   TM362900
> PC   NR35 1TL

START

Tally Ho Antiques, Mettingham, on the B1062 Bungay to Beccles road, about 1 mile East of Bungay, close to the church. Go past the shelter and information board in the lay-by, detailing the long and interesting history of the village. Cross Rectory Lane, walking on the broad verge back in the direction of Bungay, and passing a row of cottages on your right. Turn left on Vicarage Lane, at a postbox in the hedge. Carry on, passing a row of bungalows on your left, overlooking a large field with distant views, before turning off left on the Angles Way (signposted) where it becomes a footpath, after the last house.

When this path reaches a road, turn right and then immediate left at the Angles Way sign. This soon becomes a broader, tree-lined bridleway, making for pleasant walking. After about ½ mile, turn right at a minor road, soon passing by farm buildings and silos, followed by the fenced off walls of Mettingham Castle *(1) to your left, sometimes with sheep grazing. Shortly afterwards you will see the turreted gatehouse and a fine detached house, The Lodge. Stay on this road, and at a 3-way junction head in the direction signposted "Mettingham ¾".

Now on Rectory Lane, keep straight ahead, passing the Angles Way sign where you were earlier. Soon you will see the round church tower ahead, to your right. Carry on past the Old Rectory and village hall. When you reach a junction, turn right to return to the Tally Ho. A short way beyond the layby and antiques centre, on the RHS, is the entrance to All Saints church *(2), well worth a visit, in its tranquil, wooded setting.

NOTES
1. Mettingham Castle was originally the home of Sir John de Norwich, who was an admiral under Edward III. In 1342 he was given permission to convert the house into a fortified castle, as a reward for loyalty. In 1390 it was taken over as a college for priests from nearby Raveningham. This was dissolved in 1542 by Henry VIII. The castle is now privately owned, and The Lodge has holiday accommodation.
2. All Saints Mettingham is one of around 38 intact round tower churches in Suffolk (compared to Norfolk's 124). It is a grade 1 listed Norman church, restored in 1898. It has a particularly peaceful and secluded setting.

Mettingham Castle

METTINGHAM CASTLE **59**

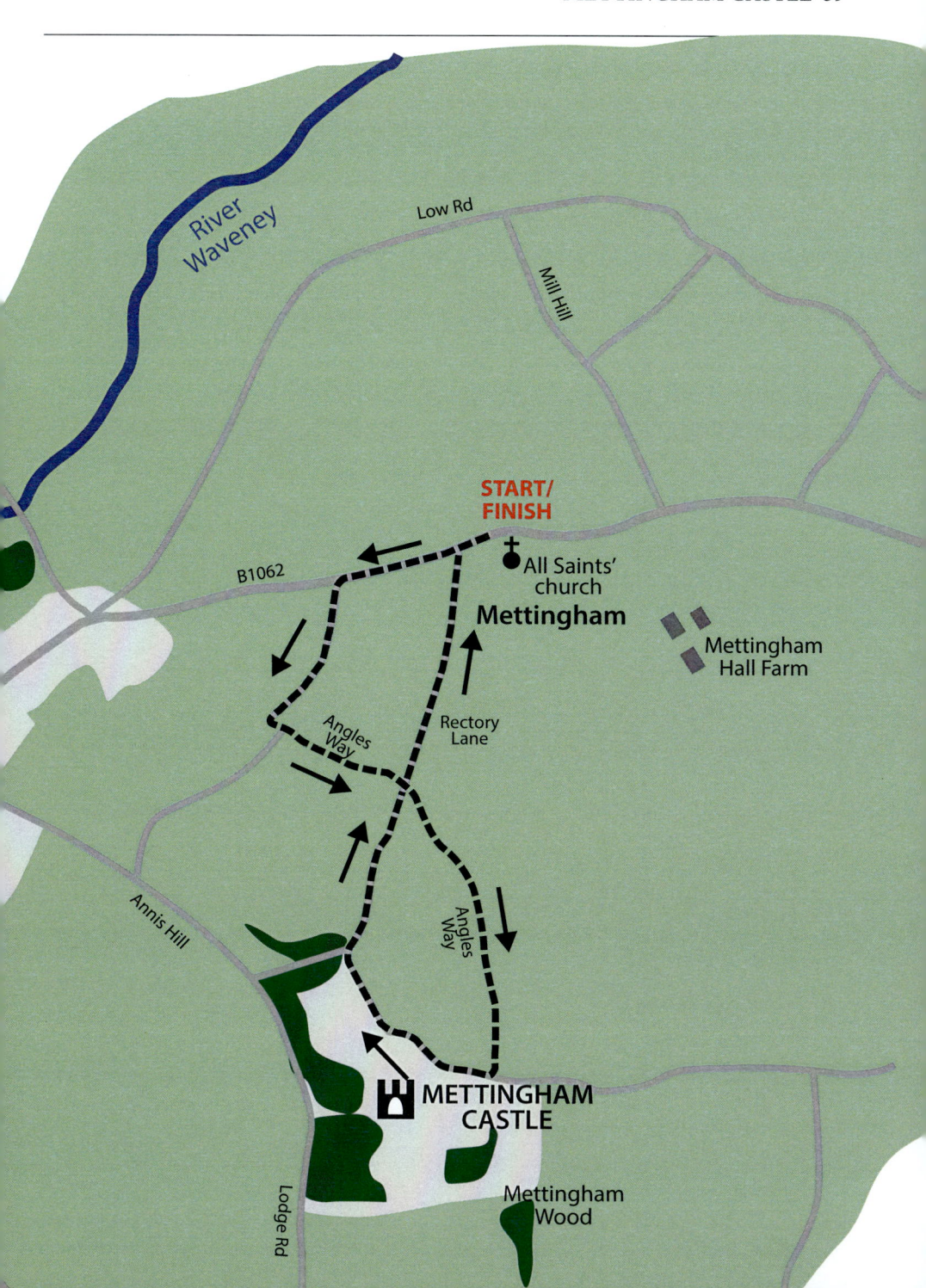

16. Ilketshall St Andrew and St John

This walk takes in four of the commons which are a distinctive feature of this area, itself a County Wildlife site and area of historical importance. A very enjoyable and varied walk in a unique and historic landscape, with an open and expansive atmosphere all of its own.

Distance 2 miles.
Terrain Signed footpaths, minor roads, common.
Refreshments Nearby Bungay has an excellent selection of cafes, pubs and restaurants.

MAP OS Explorer 231
GR   TM382866
PC   NR34 8HZ

START
Approximately 2½ miles SE of Bungay, on Holden's Common, off the A144 to Halesworth *(1) The walk starts, at the St Andrew's village sign, on a small green with hexagonal seat, at a 4 way junction close to the water tower, which is easily spotted. Head off, with the water tower to your left, down Great Common Lane, passing cowsheds and a farmhouse.

Take a left turn here at wooden posts, onto Great Common *(2). The path skirts the common, or part of it at least, with trees to your left and passing a pond to your right. Keep to this perimeter path right round this part of the common, soon, having turned back on yourself, with views ahead to the church.

Turn right where the track meets a road, and then left onto School Rd, passing the village hall on your right, and then a pond. You may want to stop to explore the beautiful church of St Andrew *(3) with its octagonal-topped round tower. At the rear of the church you will see a public FP sign pointing across a field. Take this path, which will eventually come out onto a road (Mill Lane). Turn right here, at Meadowsweet House and pond.

Just after the house, running alongside the road on the LHS, you can pick up a signposted FP along the edge of Blacksmiths Common. When you come to a 3-way junction ahead, turn right onto Clarke's Lane, signposted Halesworth and Ringsfield. Soon you will come to the charming flint-

ILKETSHALL ST ANDREW AND ST JOHN **61**

faced St Andrew's Methodist Church, on your left. Carrying on, you will reach a junction with a postbox and houses set back around a common. This is now Tooks/Little Common. Keep straight ahead on Tooks Common Lane, to wind back to the starting point on Holden's Common.

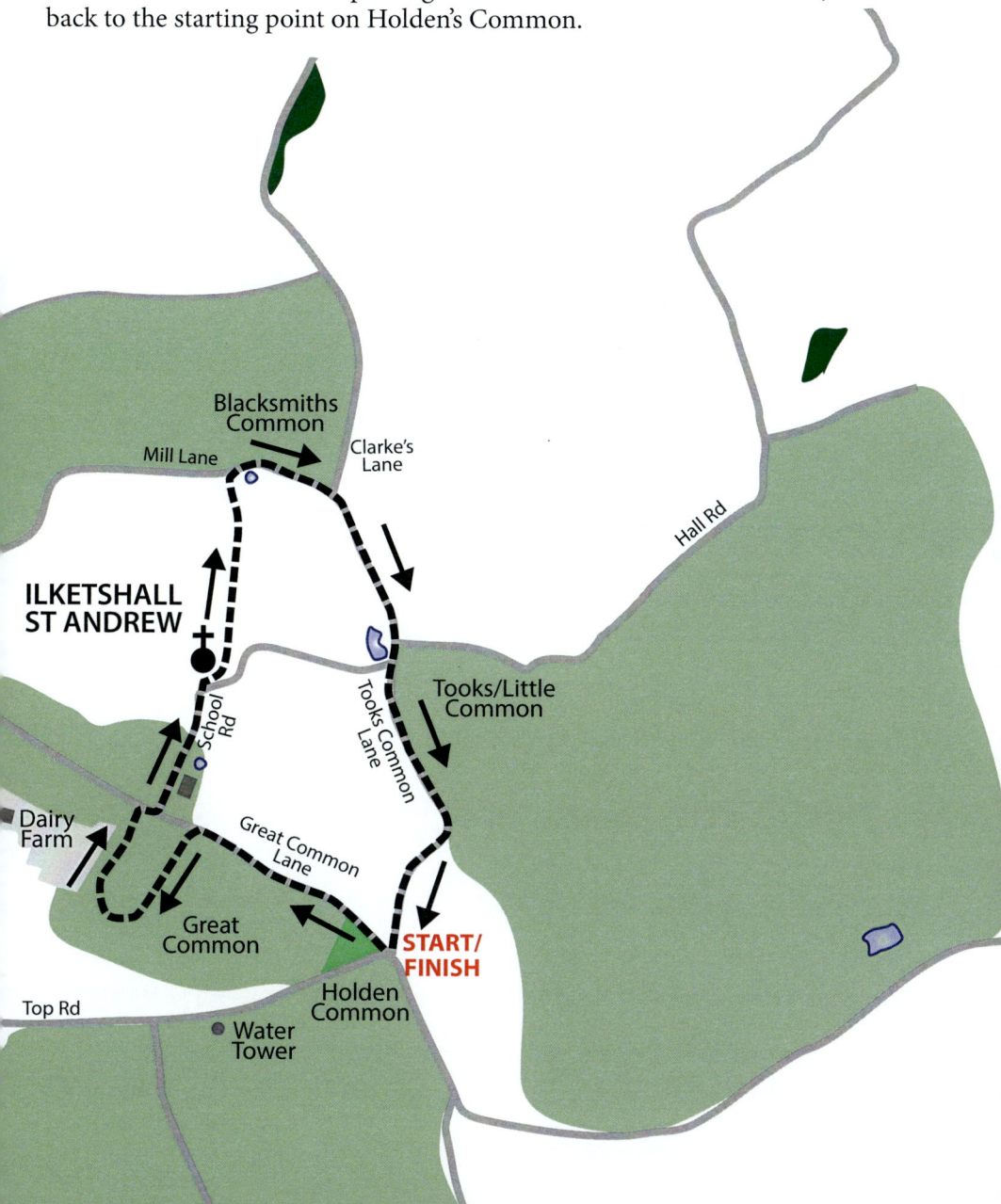

Ilketshall St Andrew

NOTES
1. The modern A144 largely follows the route of the old Roman road called Stone Street, from Halesworth to Bungay and beyond, into Norfolk.
2. The commons here encompass an area of approximately 100 acres. Most commons in England and Wales are owned, and have developed from unused or waste land. The commons of St Andrew and St John are different however in that they have no known owner. The rights of the commoners here are restricted specifically to grazing. Commons are often to be found, and survive, where land is too boggy for ploughing, which is generally the case here. To illustrate the point, there are here two "carnsers" – a Norfolk and Suffolk dialect word for a raised stone path over wet ground – used by villagers for getting to school or church. The County Wildlife Site is closely monitored by Suffolk Wildlife Trust and Natural England.
3. The church of St Andrew is of great antiquity. It was recorded in the Domesday Book of 1086. Twelfth and fourteenth century wall paintings were discovered in 2001 during restoration work.

17. *Ellingham Mill and Wardley Hill*

Ellingham is a Waveney Valley village of two distinct halves, each of great interest in its own way. This route explores both, taking in the historic mill and riverside settlement, as well as the harmonious blend of woods, parkland, farmsteads and village on the Western side.

Distance 4½ miles.
Terrain Footpaths, cycle path, minor roads, pavement through village.
Refreshments The Artichoke, Broome is the nearest hostelry, about a mile from Ellingham West. It is a pleasingly old fashioned CAMRA award winning village pub, with secluded beer garden.

MAP OS Explorer OL40
GR TM366919
PC NR35 2EP

START
The crossroads by St Mary's church, Ellingham East. (Ellingham is divided into East and West, either side of the A145. These are signposted). From the church, follow the sign to Ellingham Mill, on the river – a short walk. The mill *(1) is situated on a quite complex confluence of waterways, with very attractive riverside buildings in an atmospheric setting.

After exploring here, from the mill to the weir on the Waveney a little further along, head back towards the church, and take the first left after the mill (Old Station Lane) with views over the marshes. Soon you will turn left at the junction by the Old Station House *(2). Follow this minor road past Station Barn Farm and John William House.

At a No Through Road sign (except cycles) keep straight ahead, on the cycle track, and cross over the A143 onto Old Yarmouth Rd, shortly turning right onto a cycle track through woods. When you come out onto the A143, after ¼ mile or so, turn left on Wardley Hill Rd. Follow this winding lane uphill, passing houses and then a campsite *(3) on your RHS, to a wooded road junction.

Turn left here, signposted "Broome and Bungay", now on Old Bungay Rd, a very attractive, tree-lined lane. After about ½ mile, at a 4 way junction (and

Ellingham Mill

ignoring a turn off to the right shortly before), carry straight on onto Rectory Rd. You will now see the remote and isolated church of St Michael, Broome, ahead and to your right. Carry on for approx. one third of a mile. Before reaching as far as the track leading to the church, look out for a FP sign in the hedge, on your left, at an old fashioned metal kissing gate. Follow this grassy FP through several more such gates, for about ½ mile through attractive, landscaped parkland.

When the path comes out onto Loddon Road, turn left past Ivy House Farm, and then right on Home Farm Road. Follow this winding road for approx. ½ mile, past a pond and then Home Farm itself. At a junction, turn left carrying on into and through the village of Ellingham (West) along its main street, and back to the A143. Cross over to the cycle track opposite, and then retrace your steps back to the starting point, past Station Barn Farm.

NOTES

1. The first known reference to a mill here was in circa 1200. The present day white weather boarded mill and miller's house are C18th. Ellingham mill and sluice mark the beginning of the tidal section of the River Waveney.
2. The Old Station House, Ellingham, Norfolk, now much altered, is a former railway station. It was opened in 1863 as part of the Waveney Valley Line which ran between Tivetshall in Norfolk and Beccles in Suffolk. It was closed to passengers in 1953, and fully closed in 1965.
3. Wardley Hill Campsite is a unique and delightful 6 acre site of seemingly wild

meadow, run on carefully managed and thought out ecological principles. Highly recommended.

In the vicinity ... Broome Heath, to the Southwest, is an extensive area of gorse, heathland and attractive lakes/gravel pits, popular with walkers, picnickers and anglers. Significant Neolithic remains dating back more than 2,000 years have been unearthed here, including long barrows, earthworks, storage pits, querns and other items.

18. *Ringsfield*

A pleasantly undulating figure of eight walk, mostly on bridleways, and centred on the charming All Saints church in the secluded, characterful older part of the village. Open views, scenic hillsides; some grand old buildings.

Distance 2½ miles.
Terrain Bridleway, footpaths, minor road.
Refreshments The Horseshoes Inn, Cromwell Rd, Ringsfield, has a restaurant and outdoor seating area (*See Note 1, below*).

MAP OS Explorer 231
GR TM403884
PC NR34 8JU

START

All Saints Church, Church Lane, Ringsfield *(1), a mile or so SW of Beccles, off the A116 (Parking in layby in front of church). At the 3 way crossroads by the church *(2) follow the bridleway sign, also signed "Old Hall and Robin's Barn". Carry on past houses, and at a fork, carry straight on past a barn with a sign saying "Bridleway – farm vehicles only". After about half a mile, turn left at another bridleway sign by a concrete bridge, heading uphill.

Towards the top of the hill, by a wood, the path turns left and after a short while left again, at a junction of FPs. Follow this new section as it heads gradually round to the right, bearing slightly right at a FP sign to the right of some trees (no horses beyond this point!) and then sharp right again at the field edge. Stay on this path, around the perimeter of the field, ignoring a path to your right, and gradually dropping down to Church Rd. At a FP sign, cross a ditch and turn left onto the minor road. This will bring

Barsham, Holy Trinity

RINGSFIELD **67**

you back to the church, passing the Manor House and stately Old Rectory on your left.

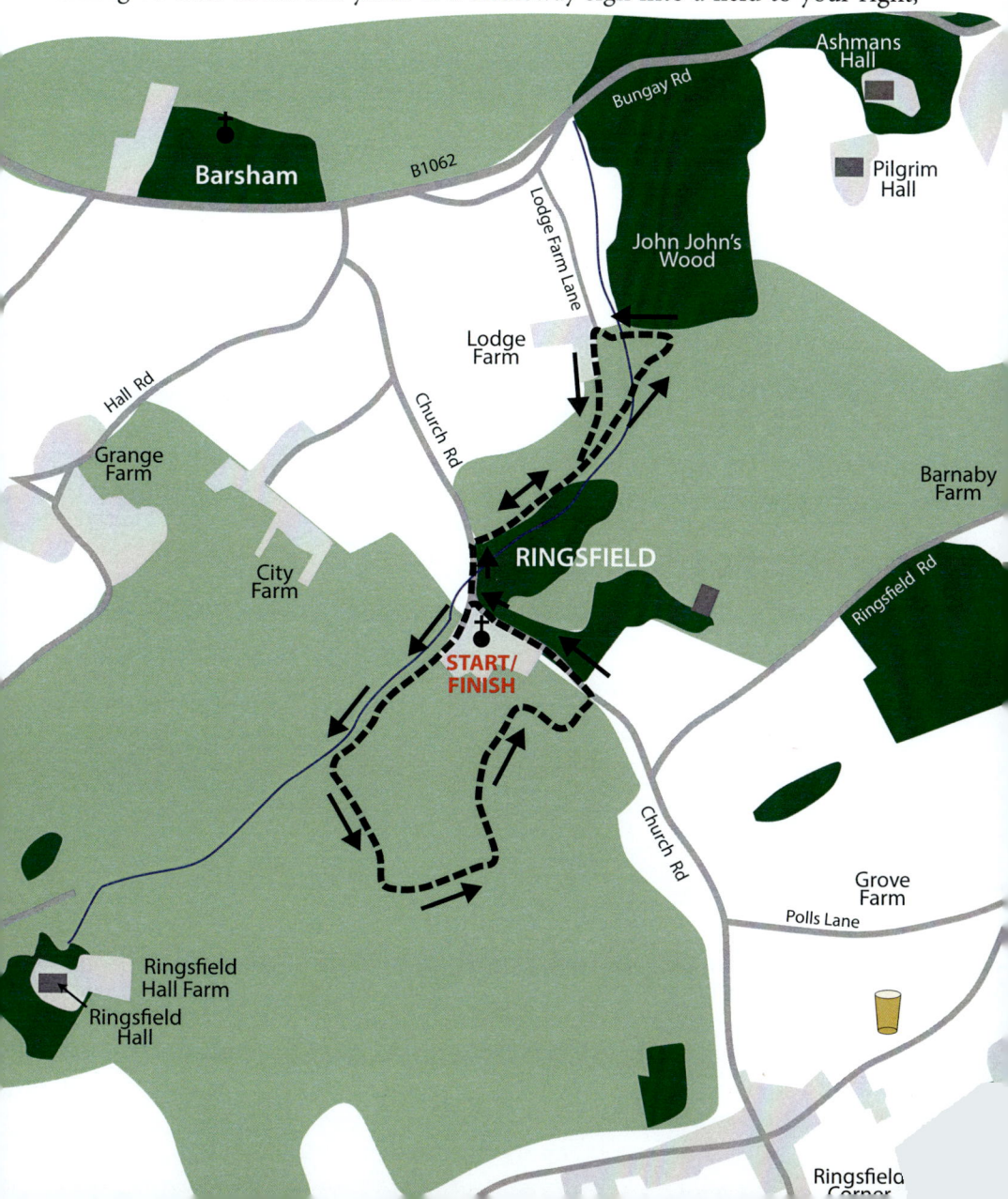

Back at the church, stay on the same road, but bear right at the junction, turning off after about 150 yards at a bridleway sign into a field to your right, following a grassy track with attractive landscaped parkland/hillside to your RHS. After approx. ¼ mile, follow a yellow FP sign to your right, then immediately left after crossing a concrete bridge. The path here runs between a stream and a fence. Follow the fence and path around to the right, and skirt along the edge of a field, heading uphill.

After 300 yds or so, turn left at a red and white pole and further FP/Bridleway signs on a fence. Double back, on the bridleway track, with a metal fence high up to your right and carry on. The track before long turns left as you approach some farm buildings, and soon rejoins the path you started on at the concrete bridge. Retrace your steps to the road, and turn left back to the church.

NOTES
1. Ringsfield is a village of two distinct halves. The original village, which this walk explores, is centred around the church and a number of grand older houses and their grounds. It is set in a very attractive wooded vale. The majority of the houses, the village green and pub are to be found about a mile to the south around the crossroads, known as Ringsfield Corner.
2. The thatched church of All Saints church Ringsfield, with its idyllic churchyard and setting, makes for a delightful starting point to the walk. Medieval in origin, and with a tower dating from 1450, it was substantially rebuilt in the 1880s by William Butterworth.

In the vicinity... Don't miss the opportunity to visit nearby Holy Trinity church, Barsham, about a mile away. It is at the end of a narrow lane, signposted off the B1062, but easily missed. The setting alone is idyllic – an enclosed, verdant meadow where time appears to have stood still. The church, likewise, has a very special atmosphere. Round towered (possibly Saxon) and with a Gothic revival interior, it appears medieval but is largely the work of Stuart rector Robert Fleming, in 1633. It has a unique East window of trellis work.

Also unique are the spring and autumn equinox events in March and September. Following repairs to the tower, it was discovered in the 1990s that at these precise times, the sun shines through the inner and outer tower windows and illuminates, on the rood screen, the figure of Christ on the cross. It is a remarkable sight. See local press for precise dates/times.

Rectory Paddock, adjacent to the church, was the location of four of the annual Barsham Fayres in the 1970s – legendary and fondly remembered East Anglian free festivals of the period.

19. Geldeston – byways and waterways

A shortish but very enjoyable walk on some of the footpaths leading from St Michael's church down into the charming village and back, by way of The Wherry Inn, Big Row and The Street, all well worth a visit or longer linger – it's that kind of place. The walk can easily be extended by way of the moorings and along the river.

Distance 2 miles, but can be extended (recommended) as below.
Terrain Footpaths, bridleway, pavement, minor road, towpath.
Refreshments The Wherry Inn; The Locks Inn *(2). Both have large gardens and restaurants, both very agreeable places to relax, inside or out.

MAP   OS Explorer OL40
GR   TM394922
PC   NR34 OLR

START

From St Michael's church *(1) car park, head up to the graveyard to find a metal kissing gate by a yew tree and grave of Oswold Etheridge. Through this gate, and at the end of a smaller graveyard, is another wooden gate. Once through this gate, head downhill to another metal gate and then bear right. Turn right again at a house (Farthing Green) and follow this path. When you come to a road (Heath Rd.) cross over and carry on. It can get a little overgrown here! This will come out onto a road, where you need to turn left and fairly soon left again down Geldeston Hill.

At the crossroads at the bottom of the hill, turn left on The Street, passing a fine crinkle crankle wall on RHS, and The Wherry Inn on your left – two characteristic features of the Norfolk/Suffolk landscape in close proximity. At the telephone box by the Dutch gable end of the village hall, turn right and follow this road (Big Row) as it curves round.

NB The walk can fairly easily and enjoyably be extended at this point, along the river (Geldeston Dyke at first). At the village hall, instead of staying on Big Row, keep straight on towards Rowancraft (an excellent centre for hiring canoes incidentally). Before you get to Rowancraft, take a FP to your left, through woods. This will soon bring you to the towpath, where you head left, under a bridge, for as far as you wish. Be aware that the towpath can get waterlogged in winter.

River Waveney at Geldeston Lock

Otherwise, follow Big Row around until it rejoins The Street. Turn right here and stay on the pavement through the village, eventually passing Dunburgh Farm on RHS, with its farm shop and paddocks. At Snakes Lane, after the farm, turn left following a public bridleway sign uphill. Back at Farthing Green, turn right on a FP, this time taking the right fork uphill on the bridleway, passing a smallholding with hens on your left. When you come out at a road, turn left to head back down to the church.

NOTES
1. St. Michael's Geldeston is a small, Norman church in a very pleasant hilly setting. It has a round tower, fairly extensively remodelled in the 1860s, and a fine late medieval porch.
2. The unique and very atmospheric Locks Inn is at the other end of the village, signposted and down a long and fairly rough (but driveable) track across the grazing marshes. It is now owned and run by the local community, and is without doubt worth the detour.

Watch out for upcoming music and events. It has a large garden adjacent to the river and recently restored lock chamber. Nearby Susan Ellis Wood is owned by the River Waveney Trust. A ferry service, the Big Dog Ferry, runs from here to the Lido at Beccles and back, a distance of 3 miles, Easter onwards.

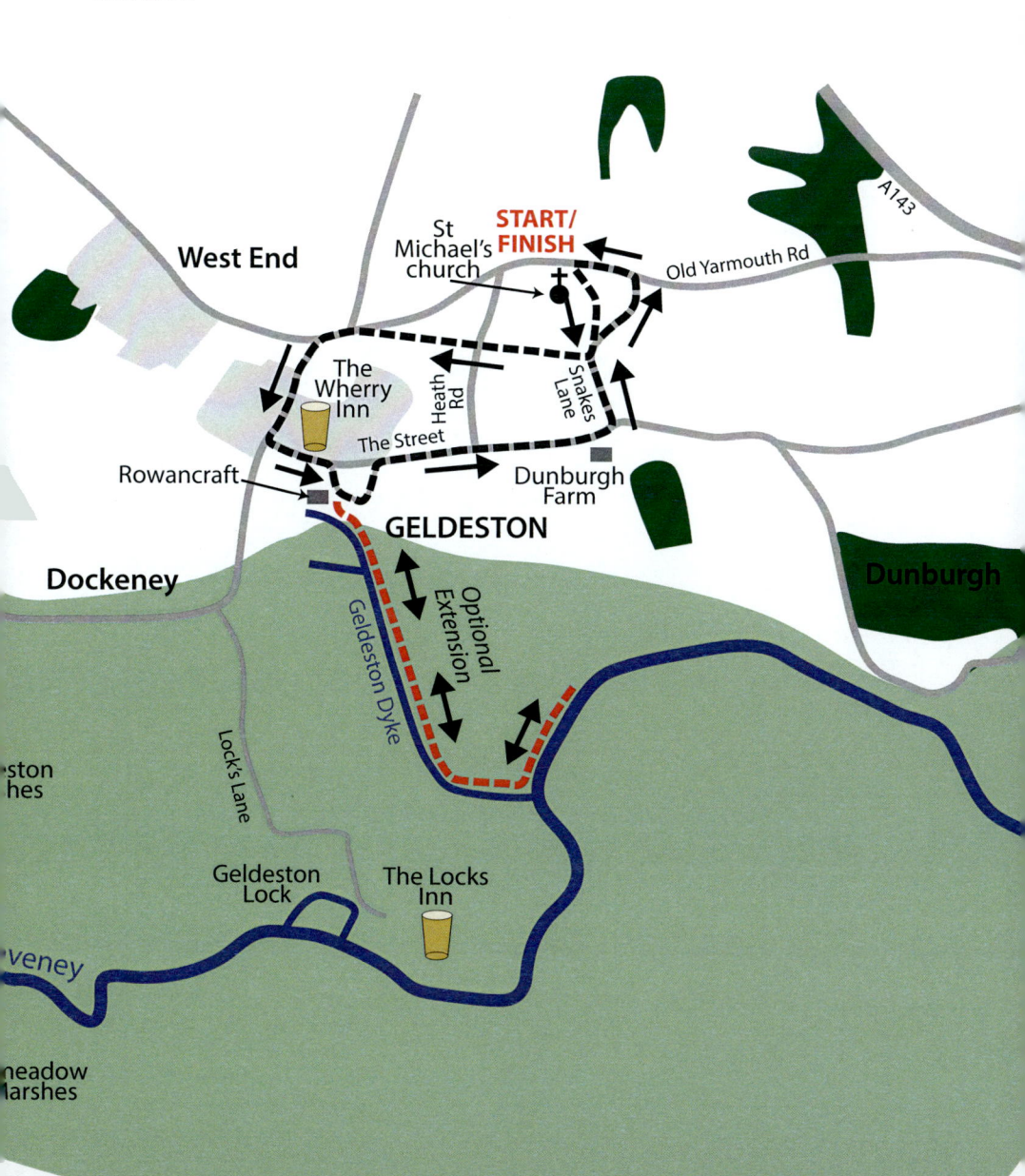

FOUR
Beccles to the Coast

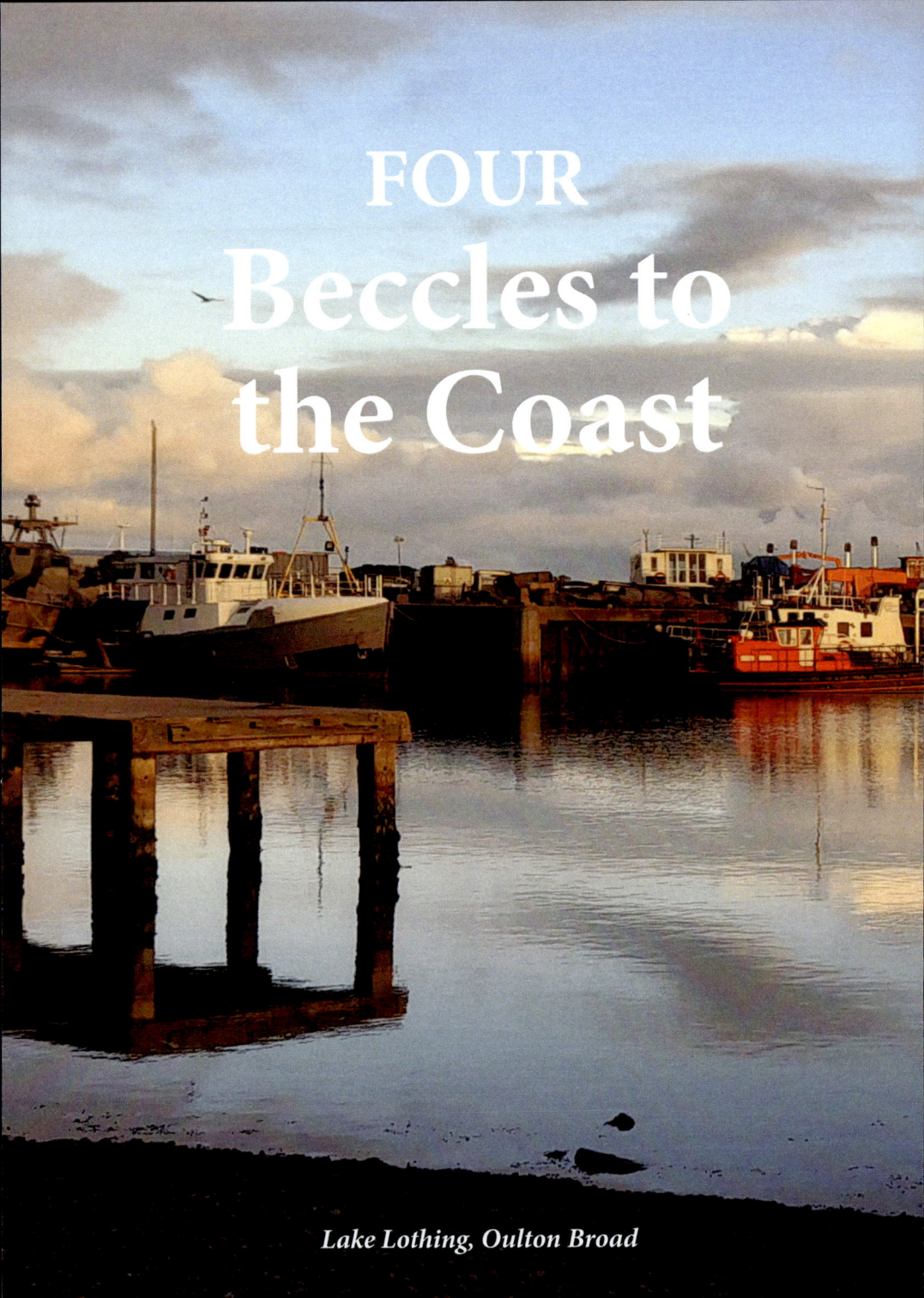

Lake Lothing, Oulton Broad

20. Chedgrave Common and Wherryman's Way

A different river (The Chet) and a section of a different long distance path, this walk also takes in Chedgrave's churchyard, common, boatyards and marina, with the attractions of adjacent Loddon and its harmonious townscape within easy walking distance.

Distance 2½ miles, with a visit to the village of Loddon.
Terrain Marked footpaths, including riverside section of Wherryman's Way, minor roads.
Refreshments The White Horse Chedgrave has a restaurant and large pleasant garden and outdoor seating area. There is a good variety of other cafes, pubs and eating places to choose from in Loddon.

MAP OS Explorer OL40
GR TM362993
PC NR14 6NH

START

All Saints church, Hardley Rd, Chedgrave. There is a car park here, as well as a playground and seating, within an attractive undulating setting. Carry on walking down Hardley Rd, away from the shops and church, for about a quarter of a mile, passing Pits Lane on your right. Turn right at a sign for Chedgrave Common and Wherryman's Way *(1). After about half a mile on this unmade up road, you will see a wooden gate on your RHS leading onto the common. Head this way, across the tussocky common towards houses until you come to another FP sign by the River Chet.

Turn right at the gate here and follow the riverside path for roughly half a mile, with extensive marshes and reedbeds to your right. When the path turns inland, near boatyards, go through another gate and then turn left almost immediately on a permissive path to the rear of the boatyards. This path soon heads into woods before emerging into more boatyards. Keep straight ahead, and you will come out onto a main road by attractive allotments, Loddon Mill *(2) Bridge Stores, and boat moorings – a great place to take a pause and enjoy the riverside surroundings.

River Chet, Chedgrave

Where Chedgrave finishes, Loddon begins. At this point therefore you may want to head up Bridge St to explore the town before carrying on. There are many handsome Georgian and Victorian houses and buildings along the way, and in the centre of town Holy Trinity church sits in the midst of an especially beautiful and extensive churchyard.

Back at the bridge, carry on, away from the Mill, and into Chedgrave, passing by cottages and houses before bearing right onto Langley Rd, just before The White Horse pub. Soon you will arrive back at the parade of shops, turning right again at Hardley Rd and returning to All Saints church.

NOTES
1. The Wherryman's Way is a 35 mile long distance path running from Norwich to Great Yarmouth. It is named after the flat bottomed sailing barges, distinctive to Norfolk and Suffolk, that used to carry cargo up and down the River Yare and other rivers and waterways in the region. The path follows the course of the Yare where possible, but does also follow the Chet upstream to Loddon.
2. The mill at Loddon was sometimes known as Chedgrave Mill, and is one of the earliest recorded buildings in the town. Although recorded in the Domesday Book, the present mill, near the staithe, was built in the 1700s. It is considered to be the oldest in East Anglia, and the only all timber mill in England.

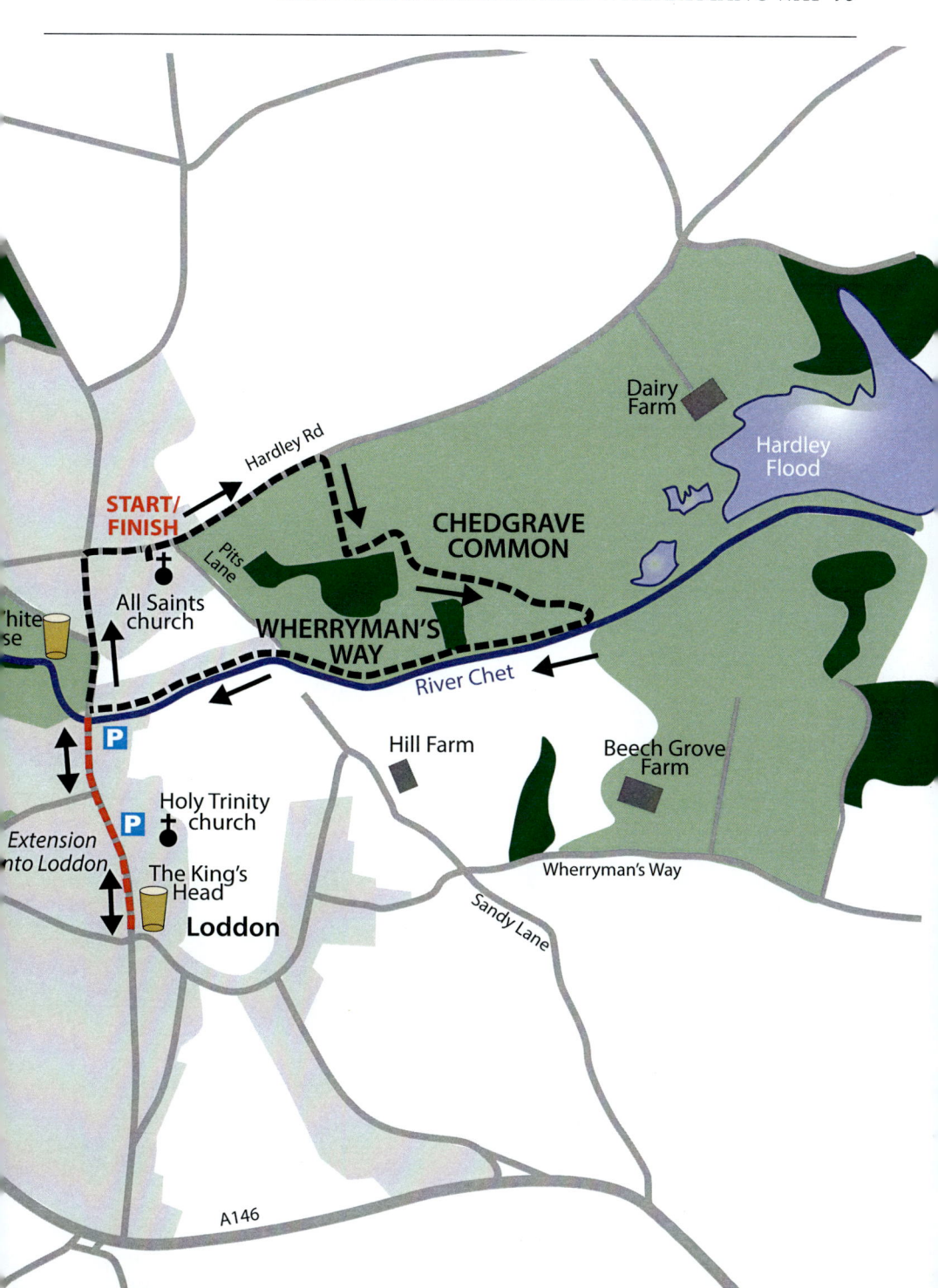

CHEDGRAVE COMMON AND WHERRYMAN'S WAY 75

21. *Dunburgh and Beccles riverside*

From Gillingham, uphill to the charming village of Dunburgh, this invigorating riverside walk winds downwards to the north bank of the Waveney, before heading towards and then alongside the town of Beccles, with fine views, before crossing Beccles Marshes to return.

Distance Shorter option 2½ miles. Longer option 3½ miles.
Terrain Minor village roads through Dunburgh and Gillingham; pavement on return stretch; marked footpaths. NB the riverside paths can get very waterlogged in winter months.
Refreshments The Swan Motel, Gillingham; good range of cafes, pubs and restaurants in the centre of Beccles. The Waveney House Hotel, Puddingmoor, Beccles, has a very attractive riverside terrace, with adjacent conservatory restaurant if the weather is inclement.

MAP OS Explorer OL40
GR TM412916
PC NR34 0LD

START
The Swan Motel in Gillingham, NW of Beccles. Turn left after The Swan onto The Street, then left again on Kings Dam. Follow this road around and through the village, passing a recreation ground on your RHS. Leaving Gillingham, you will start to climb uphill to the hamlet of Dunburgh, passing Manor House Farm on your left and a postbox to your right. Just beyond a house called Dunburgh Wood you will see a FP sign to your left, just before a lay-by.

Take this path, which soon becomes a set of steps, with wooden handrail, leading down into the wood. At the bottom of these steps, turn left following a FP sign into woods, with a house high above to your left. Soon you will be on a path with the River Waveney now visible to your

Dunburgh riverside

DUNBURGH AND BECCLES RIVERSIDE 77

right. Stay on this path. After about 1 mile you will be able to see the tower of Beccles church *(1) up ahead. As you approach the town *(2) you will begin to see moored boats, and boathouses on the opposite bank.

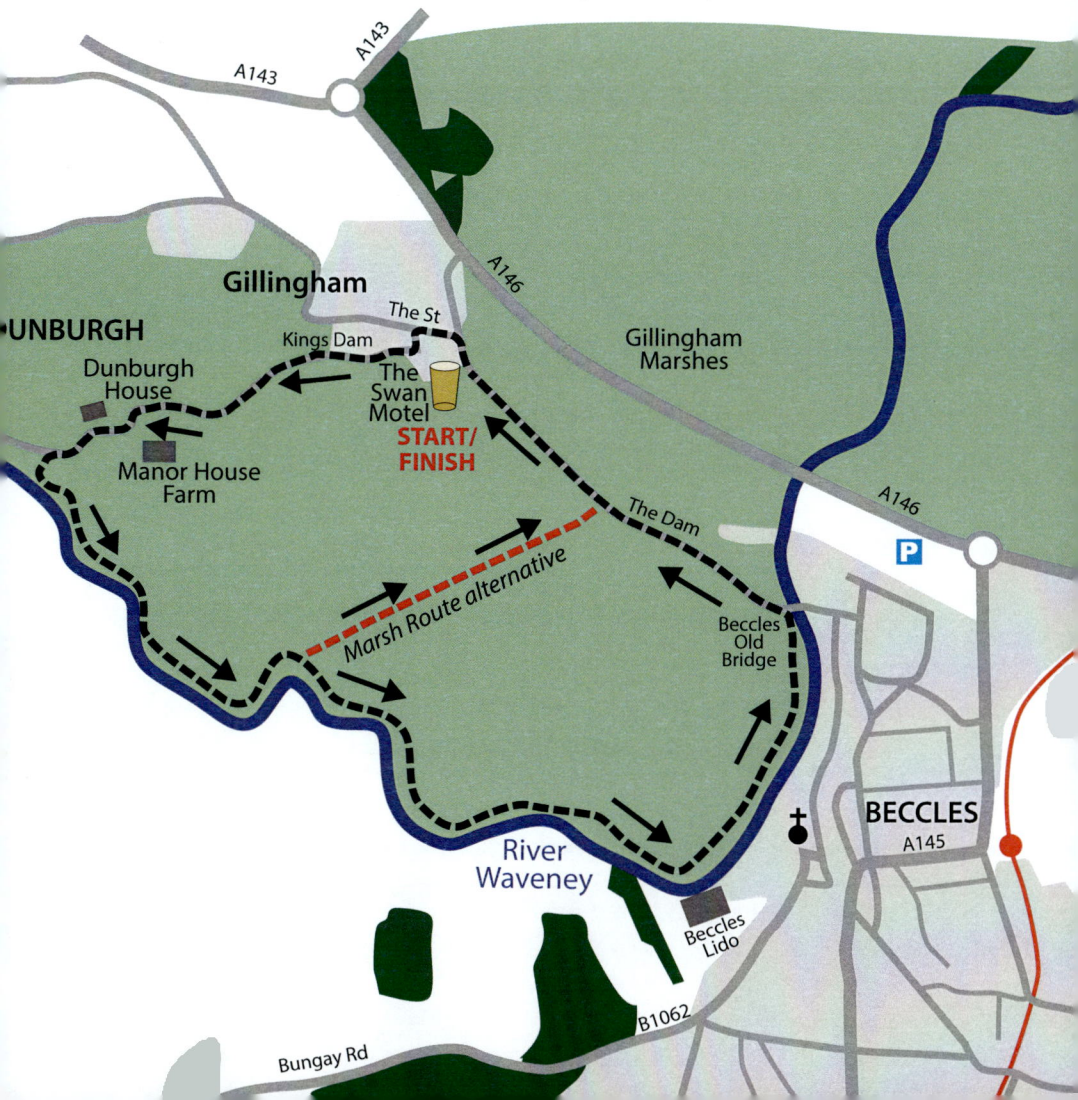

At this point you have a choice. You can either a) stay on this path by the river as it turns to the North, passing Beccles Lido *(3) on the opposite bank, and a succession of attractive gardens sloping down to the river from the town above. This is a longer option (see below) enabling you to see more of the river and town from this vantage. The riverside path will bring you out at Beccles Old Bridge onto a road called The Dam. Turning left here you will need to follow this road, on the pavement, back into Gillingham, a distance of about ¾ mile.

Alternatively, b), you can turn left away from the river heading down a slope to a metal gate and following a long straight track (Marsh Route) at right angles to the river across the marshes, with a dyke to your RHS. You will pass through two further gates before coming out onto the same road, The Dam, where you turn left and follow the pavement back into the village of Gillingham.

Beccles Lido

NOTES
1. St Michael's, Beccles, is a church on a grand scale. It is unusual (there is only one other in Suffolk) in having a tower which is separate from the body of the church. It rises nearly 100ft above sea level. The views westward from the churchyard are superb and far reaching, over the river and beyond to the surrounding countryside.
2. Beccles itself is a unique and characterful town, and well worth taking the time to explore. With its wealth of historic buildings and advantageous location, it is also a major boating centre at the Southern edge of the Broads National Park. A walk from New Market in the centre of town, down to the Quay by way of Saltgate and then Northgate, with its distinctive narrow "scores" leading down to the river, will enable you to see what makes the town so special. The scores were used for landing herrings a millennium ago. The street names themselves hint at the town's Scandinavian past – 'gade' is Danish for 'street'. On Northgate alone you will see elegant Georgian town houses, Dutch gables, fanlights and porticos, side by side with modest cottages, old maltings and signs for other trades of the past, all harmoniously blended.
3. Beccles Lido is highly recommended – a much loved, heated (to 28 C in the summer season) outdoor swimming pool in an idyllic location on the banks of the River Waveney. It is relaxed and traditional in style, with a 30 metre pool, diving boards, a grassy outdoor seating and sunbathing area and a café. It is one of a kind. The Big Dog Ferry, a 1950s former lifeboat, runs a regular passenger service covering the 3 miles from the landing stage by the Lido to Geldeston Lock and back, along the Waveney.

22. Burgh St Peter Staithe and Carlton Marshes

A walk of two connected halves. The first (which is deliberately short to allow time for the second) is in and around the Staithe and the Waveney River Centre on the Northern side. A short foot ferry crossing from here takes you over to the 1,000 plus acres of the magnificent Carlton Marshes Nature Reserve, with its enticing network of footpaths – the second part.

Distance 1 mile (Part 1). Variable, according to preference (Part 2).
Terrain Marked footpaths and minor roads (Part 1); footpaths, some gravelled (Part 2).
Refreshments The Waveney Inn and shop (Part 1); Carlton Marshes Visitor Centre café (Part 2).

MAP OS Explorer OL40
GR TM492934
PC NR34 ODE

START

PART ONE – Waveney River Centre (WRC) Burgh St Peter Staithe, Norfolk – follow the signs off A143 Beccles to Gt Yarmouth road, at Haddiscoe or Toft Monks. Walk out of the WRC, past the boatshed. Go straight ahead on a track, to the right of Burgh Rd, then immediate left into a field, with permissive path sign (WRC). Walk along the field edge for about 200 yds till you come to a gap in the fence, out onto a road. Cross over and pick up another path opposite, also with WRC signs. This runs between an attractive avenue of trees, with paddocks to your LHS and a field to your right.

When you come out onto another lane, with views ahead over river and marshes, turn left, overlooking chalets to your right. Follow this road back to the WRC, and then keep straight ahead on Church Lane towards the very striking ziggurat-style church tower of St Mary the Virgin *(1). After exploring the church, return the way you came, but turn left after a large white house, into the WRC. Head down along the marina to Burgh St Peter Staithe *(2), where the foot ferry leaves from. This part of the walk is roughly 1 mile.

PART TWO – Carlton Marshes *(3), by foot ferry. The Ternpike (spelling is deliberate!) runs on the hour throughout the year, from the WRC side. It can be summoned on demand, throughout the year, for the short crossing. Tel. no for ferryman is 07500 571232. WRC info is 01502 677599 – double check the times and availability of return crossings, if you are intending to return the same way, also for prices. The modern ferry has revived an ancient tradition, and in effect joins Norfolk to Suffolk.

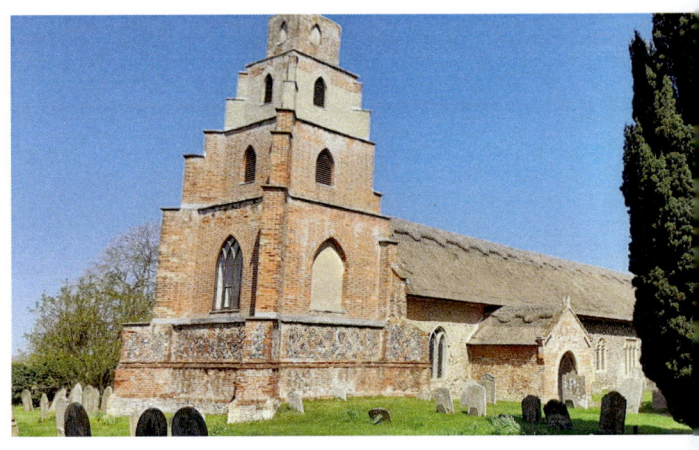

Burgh St Peter, St Mary

From the drop-off point on the other side, it is a 25/30 minute walk across the reserve to the very impressive new visitor centre and café. Turn immediate right on the path, and then left, away from the river, when you see a sign saying "Beccles Quay 7miles". Stay on this path, which is in fact a section of the Angles Way, across the middle of the marshes. Because the path is a raised causeway, you have the benefit of spectacular views across the almost 1,200 acres of the reserve. Even if you only decide to go a short way along, it is abundantly worth the trip. There is a network of other trails to explore too, as well as various hides and lookouts – pick up a leaflet at the WRC or at Carlton Marshes Visitor Centre.

NB As an alternative, you can access Carlton Marshes and the Visitor Centre from the Suffolk side, at Burnt Hill Lane, Oulton Broad (see below).

NOTES
1. The church of St Mary the Virgin dates to around 1200, with the very weird and wonderful zigurrat style tower being a late C18th addition. It is believed that Samuel Boycott, the second of five Boycott rectors of the church, was inspired on his travels by the zigurrat temples of Mesopotamia. Permission for this one was granted in 1793.
2. "Staithe" is a predominantly Norfolk word for a landing stage for boats and ships. There are many such in the Norfolk and Suffolk Broads.
3. Carlton Marshes Nature Reserve, with its well over 1,000 acres of wetland

BURGH ST PETER STAITHE AND CARLTON MARSHES 81

wilderness, and extensive network of footpaths and boardwalks, is owned and managed by Suffolk Wildlife Trust. It has benefited recently from the allocation of £4 million of Heritage Lottery Funding. The very impressive and sympathetically designed new Visitor Centre, with its shop, café, and other facilities opened in 2021. The views from the terrace are outstanding. The Centre, postcode NR33 8HU, is accessed from Burnt Hill Lane in Carlton Colville, off the A146 to Beccles. The turnoff is signposted near the Tesco Express.

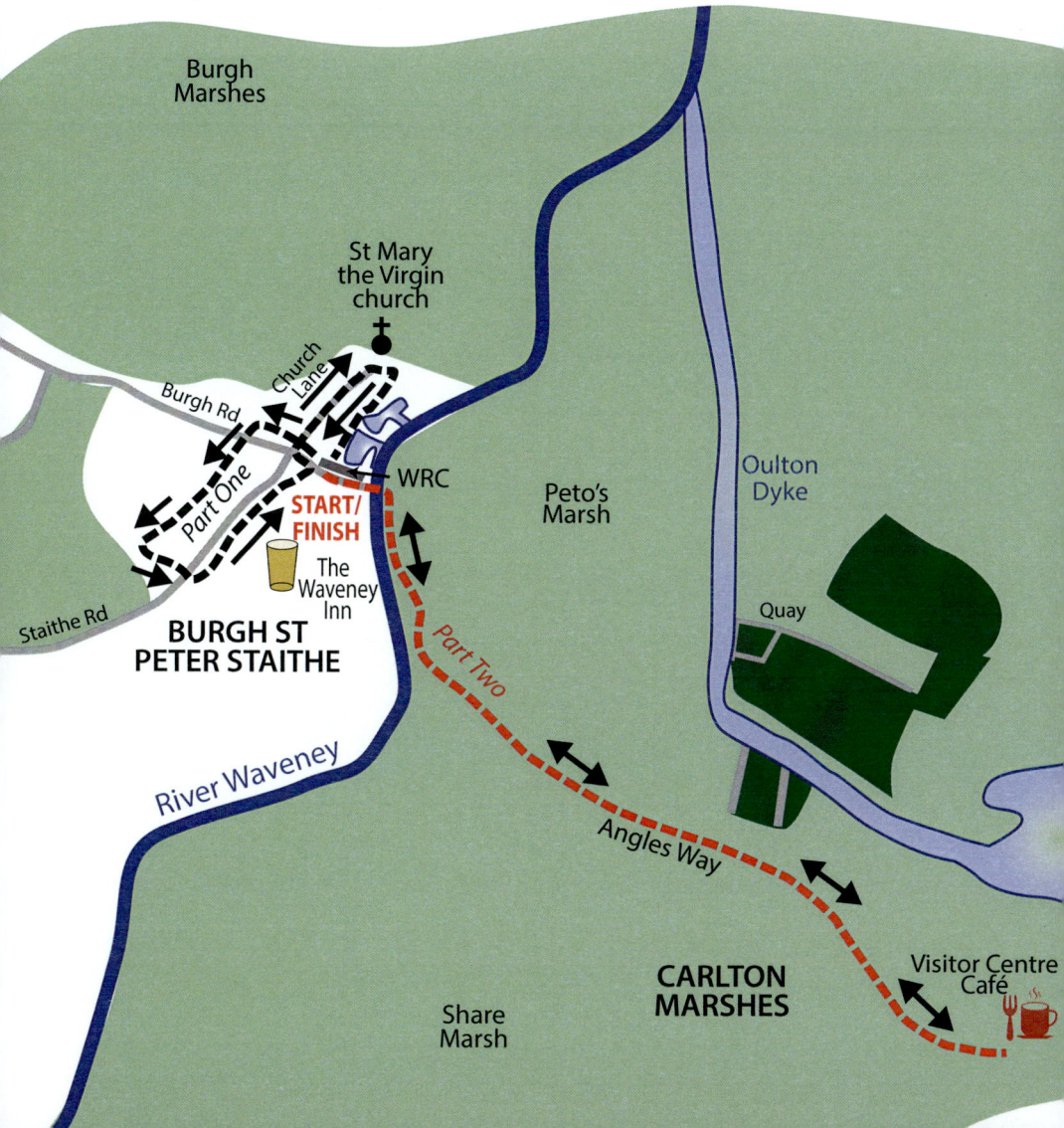

23. *Herringfleet Hills and Somerleyton Staithe*

This varied and exhilarating circular walk takes in hilly woodland, expansive reedbeds and riverside views, as well as a historic restored mill and a medieval round tower church. The magnificent Somerleyton Hall and Park adjoin the attractive village of Somerleyton.

Distance 3 miles.
Terrain Marked footpaths mostly; also minor road and B road verge (see note *3).
Refreshments Refreshments The Dukes Head, Slugs Lane, Somerleyton. Large beer garden, conservatory and restaurant.

MAP   OS Explorer OL40
GR   TM469982
PC   NR32 5QU

START

Herringfleet Hills car park, Herringfleet Rd (B1074) from St Olaves to Somerleyton. NB The entrance to the car park, which is inconspicuous and easily missed, is on the right, as you are driving from St Olaves, and about ¾ mile beyond the turnoff to Herringfleet. Check car park times before you leave – it is usually locked at 4pm, though often stays open later in summer months.

From the car park, go through a wooden gate and turn immediate right. (Following the waymarked path shown in red on the noticeboard in the car park, for this first part). Follow the path through a dense wood, soon heading downhill to your left, through ferns. At the bottom, at a clearing, the path turns left alongside the stream/dyke which is on your right hand side. You will also now see the Herringfleet Smock (drainage) mill * (1) to your right, in the distance.

Stay on this path for ¼ mile or so till the stream turns right towards the mill, at a metal gate with stile. Cross over and head towards the mill, on a footpath which follows the left hand bank of the dyke. The approach to the mill is by way of a wooden footbridge, which you need to cross. Once over the footbridge, and having explored the mill, go up four steps and turn left along a causeway with extensive reedbeds on both sides. Assuming the reeds are not too high, you may soon see the Waveney itself, a broad river at this point, on your right hand side.

Herringfleet Smock Mill

If you don't see it, you may well hear passing boats. Keep a lookout for reed buntings and warblers, the habitat here being ideal for both species.

Stay on the causeway, and about ¾ mile beyond the mill you will arrive at Somerleyton Staithe * (2). Follow the footpath, which now turns away from the river to your left, before you reach the marina and boatyards. After approx. 100yds, turn left at an electricity sub-station and follow the lane uphill, with new houses on your right. Turn left at the top, by the Dukes Head pub *(3)

Follow this winding lane (Slugs Lane) till you come to a T junction. Turn left here, walking on the roadside verge. You will soon pass a fine gabled house and an impressive historic thatched barn on your right (Manor House Farm). Not far beyond this, and on the same side of the road, you will see the beautiful and ancient church of St Margaret Herringfleet * (4). Carry on in the same direction for a little over ½ mile, on this road, back to the starting point.

NOTES
1. Herringfleet Smock Mill is a windpump or drainage mill built in the 1820s and worked by marshmen until the 1950s. Water is lifted from the dyke by the external scoopwheel. It is the last of the old wooden pumping mills in the Broads in working order. It is grade 2 listed.
2. Somerleyton Staithe is "a long, grassy riverbank flanked by marshes and wooded hills … It is a beautiful mooring overlooking one of the last remaining railway swing bridges on the Broads, built in 1905" (Norfolk Broads Direct website)

Irises, Oulton Dyke

3. NB. This walk essentially follows 4 sides of a square. The final side requires, unavoidably, walking along the verge and sometimes roadside of the B1074, so care is required. If you would prefer not to do this stretch (approx. ¾ mile) the other option is to return the way you came, for example from the Dukes Head. The total length of walk will be about the same.
4. St Margaret's Herringfleet is a medieval round tower church with some C19th restoration. It is a lovely church, inside and out, of very simple and ancient appearance, dating from before the Norman Conquest. It has a unique collection of stained glass, C14th – C18th, some of it from Cologne.

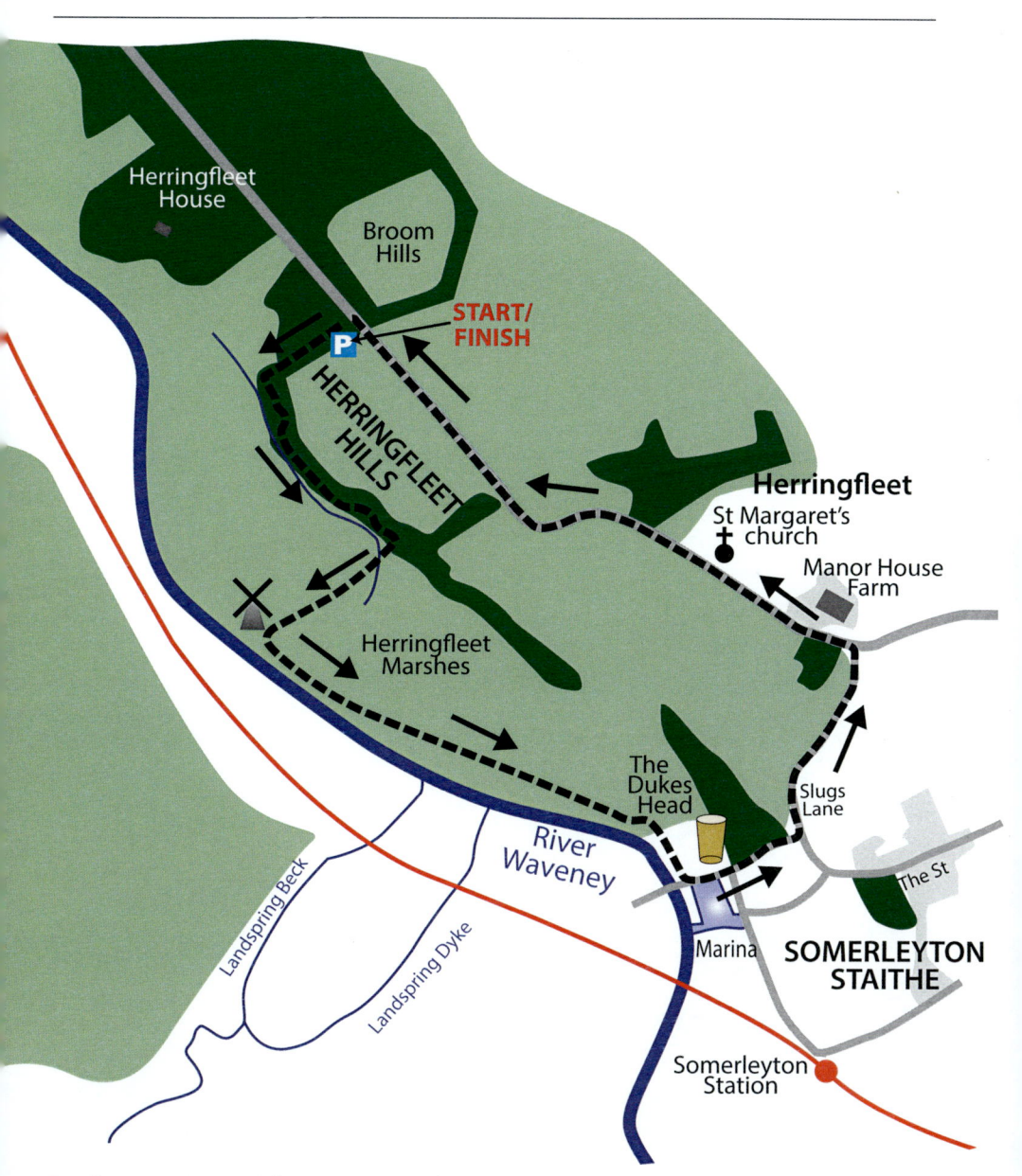

HERRINGFLEET HILLS AND SOMERLEYTON STAITHE 85

In the vicinity ... The vast Somerleyton Estate covers an area of 5,000 acres, 1,000 acres of which are now fenced and in the process of being re-wilded, under the stewardship of Hugh, the current Lord Somerleyton. Check website for details of entry to the Victorian stately home and gardens.

24. St. Olaves and Waveney Forest

Riverside moorings and boatyards, ancient forest, an Augustinian priory, a Norman round tower church, not to mention an owl sanctuary and the oldest pub in the Broads – this is a walk that will exercise your imagination as well as your legs.

> **Distance** 4 miles.
> **Terrain** Marked footpaths, including a section of the Angles Way; minor roads and tracks; short section of A143. Waterproof footwear essential – paths can be very wet, especially in winter.
> **Refreshments** The Bell Inn, St Olaves is a busy and popular pub with a large riverside seating area as well as indoor restaurant. Fritton Plant Centre has a pleasant, leafy café also. Priory Farm Restaurant is a family restaurant close to the Priory ruins, and located in a very atmospheric converted barn.
>
> **MAP** OS Explorer OL40
> **GR** TM457994
> **PC** NR31 9HG

START

The large car park at The Bell Inn, St Olaves (reputedly the oldest pub in the Broads, with parts of the building dating back to 1520). Come out of the car park, turn left and cross over the road. Just before the bridge over the Waveney *(1) turn right after Bridge Stores and take a fairly inconspicuous and narrow path by boatyards, with a low wall to your left. Follow this path, passing to the rear of several chalets and bungalows, towards the drainage mill and pumping station. Stay on the path as it veers off to the right after the moorings, towards Waveney Forest *(2).

Where the path divides, turn right, away from the river. When you reach a junction of paths, with pylons ahead, turn right into the forest, passing the gated "Roundhouse" on your left. Stay on this rising, pebbly track through silver birch and conifer woods. After about 10 minutes you will come out onto a road (New Rd) by some houses.

Turn left here, and after about ½ mile on New Road, still with the Waveney Forest to your left, turn right where the road becomes a track, passing a sign

St Olaves

for Low Farm Cottage. Shortly after Low Farm itself, turn right, following an Angles Way FP sign. Stay on this path for about ½ mile, with a succession of paddocks and stables to your left. The Angles Way path then veers off to the right before skirting along the edge of a pig farm. Keep straight ahead in the same direction, passing a house on your RHS.

When you come out onto the main road (A143) turn right, passing in front of Fritton Plant Centre and the Owl Sanctuary *(3), where you may want to pause to explore. Just beyond here, cross over the road, following signs for the church *(4) and Angles Way, and crossing cattle grids. Turn right in front of the beautiful church, again following the Angles Way sign, on a minor road between hedges. This soon brings you back to the main road, at the Fritton village sign. Carry on into the village, passing the Institute and then the Decoy Tavern on your RHS.

Just after the pavement runs out, at a telephone box and the Old School House, you will see a sign on the other side of the road saying "FP St Olaves". Cross over and take this path, staying parallel to, and above, the road, which you will eventually rejoin, by some houses. You will now need to walk on the grass verge for 200 yards or so, back into the village of St Olaves.

St Olaves Priory

Carry on past the garage and Herringfleet Rd, shortly afterwards crossing over and following a sign and grassy path the short way to St Olaves Priory (English Heritage) *(5). Return the same way to rejoin the road, and turn right, back to the Bell Inn.

NOTES

1. There are actually two bridges in close proximity here. The first, as you approach St Olaves from Haddiscoe, is over the C19th canal, the New Cut, with the railway line running beside it. The second, steel bridge, is over the Waveney and is of more recent construction, with a pedestrian walkway added in 1960.
2. The Waveney Forest, aka Fritton Wood or Fritton Warren, has a long history of military use, including during both world wars. It is a large area of coniferous woodland, including heathland and bog. With its birch carr and sphagnum bog, it provides habitat for many protected species.
3. Fritton Owl Sanctuary is a very worthwhile enterprise and a delight to visit. It was set up in 2013 to provide a home for unwanted, captive bred owls of many fascinating varieties as well as injured native species. Entrance is free, but donations are encouraged to enable the work to continue. Open every day 10-4pm.
4. The thatched, round towered church of St Edmunds, Fritton is also open 10-4 every day, and is an absolute gem. It has a unique sequence of wall paintings depicting the martyrdom of St Edmund, only discovered in 1967, and a particularly beautiful Norman chancel.
5. St Olaves Priory – "This small Augustinian priory was founded by Roger Fitz Osbert in about 1216. It is dedicated to Olaf, the C11th king and patron saint of Norway whose stark Christian message was 'baptism or death'. The

ST. OLAVES AND WAVENEY FOREST **89**

priory was dismantled in 1784. Its C14th refectory undercroft, with its vaulted brick ceiling, still almost complete, is an important early example of the use of brick in England." (english.heritage.org.uk)

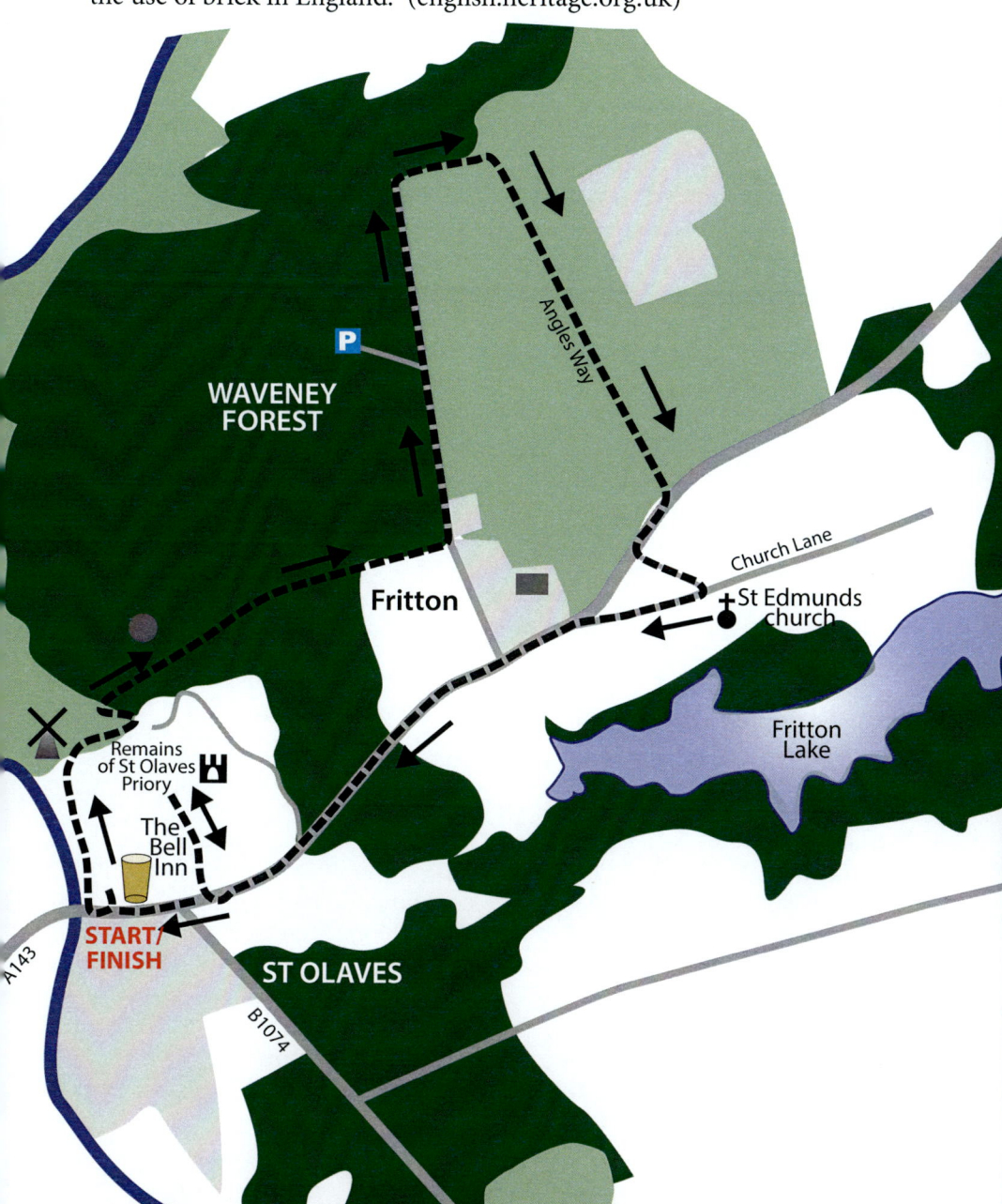

25. Oulton Marshes Nature Reserve

Close to the Eastern, seaward stretch of the Waveney, and the waterside attractions of Oulton Broad, this walk has a lot to offer – a historic church in a spectacular setting, immense skies and vistas bisected by remote-seeming rivers and rail lines, marshland paths and wildlife aplenty.

Distance 2½ miles. (NB The walk can very easily be extended, back at St Michaels church, by exploring some of the other very pleasant signposted footpaths heading off from here).

Terrain Marked footpaths, bridleways, towpath and tracks. All of these can get very waterlogged, especially in the winter months.

Refreshments Plenty to choose from in Oulton Broad, including The Wherry and The Commodore, both large pubs with restaurants overlooking the Broad. The Old Dairy is a rather special artisan coffee shop and bakery with indoor and outdoor seating, again close by the Broad. No. 142 Café and Bar, Bridge St. is likewise very agreeable.

MAP OS Explorer OL40
GR TM510935
PC NR32 3JP

River Waveney

Peto's Marsh

START

St. Michael's church *(1), Church Lane, Oulton. At the lychgate, by the main entrance to the churchyard, you will see paths heading off in various directions. Find the Suffolk Wildlife Trust information board and map here – "Welcome to Oulton Marshes Nature Reserve" *(2). This walk is similar to the one shown in red here, but half a mile or so longer. Set off from here on a bridleway, part of the Angles Way, downhill and parallel to the side of the church.

At the bottom of this hill, with the church behind you, turn left at another bridleway sign through a wooden gate with a sign that says "Bridleway only". Stay on this wooded path for ¼ mile or so until you come to a level crossing. Cross carefully over the level crossing and carry straight on. You will have

OULTON MARSHES NATURE RESERVE 91

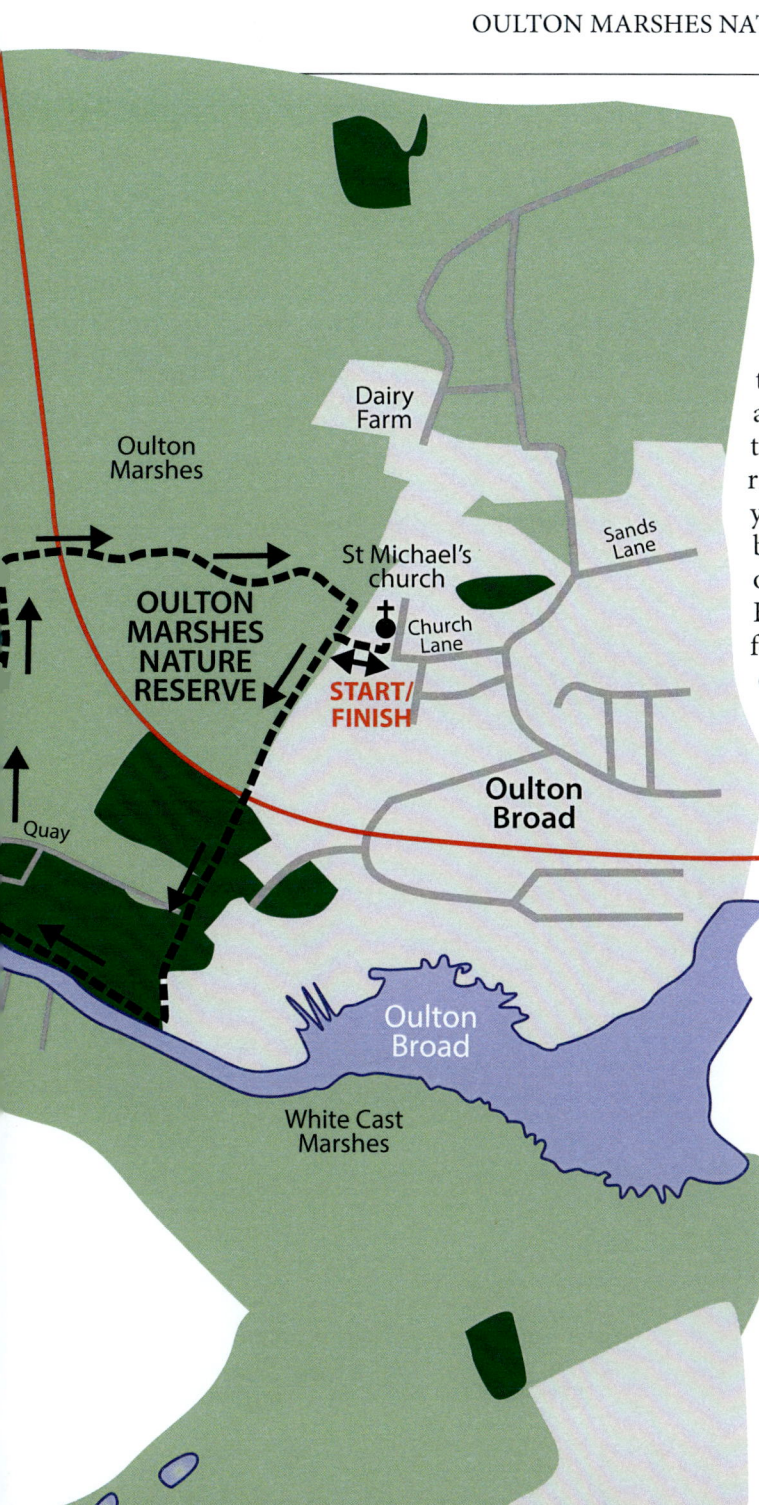

Oulton Marshes and a dyke to your right, and a fairly steep wooded bank to your left.

Carry on along this path, ignoring a FP going off to your right, at right angles, until you arrive at the broad waterway of Oulton Dyke. Bear right here, following the bank of the dyke. After about 5 minutes the dyke takes a turn to the right and you will shortly arrive at a moorings and landing stage called the "Dutch Tea Gardens". Carry on in the same direction.

After about ½ mile, and having passed a wooden viewing platform down a few steps to your right, you will come to a turnoff *(3) where you will

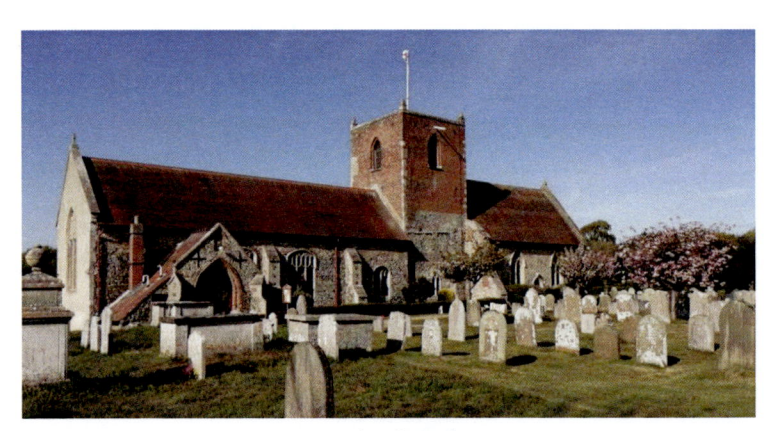

St Michael, Oulton

see the traffic light for the railway crossing ahead. Head towards this, away from the dyke, and cross over the railway line. You will have been able to make out, while walking, the tower of St Michael's church, with its flag, ahead of you in the distance. Stay on this track, with grazing marshes to both sides. When you come to a wooden gate, go through and follow the track round to the right, in the direction of the church. Fairly soon you will arrive back at the point where you turned off on the bridleway earlier. Head uphill, left, towards the church and back to the starting point.

NOTES
1. The setting of St Michael's church, on relatively high ground, is outstanding. (Churches dedicated to St Michael are very often situated on high ground). Don't miss the opportunity to take in the glorious views Westward, over Oulton Dyke and then the Waveney, to Burgh St Peter and beyond. There are benches in the churchyard here. The base of the central tower of the church is Saxon, C10th or C11th. Otherwise, most of the fabric dates from the C13th.
2. Characteristic species here include Chinese water deer, Belted Galloway cattle, mute swans, Cetti's warblers, snipe, water voles and common lizards.
3. Half a mile or so beyond this turnoff, Oulton Dyke merges with the Waveney, as it flows onward to Somerleyton, then joining with the river Yare at Breydon Water on the outskirts of Great Yarmouth.

In the vicinity ... People generally associate The Broads with Norfolk, but Oulton Broad – "The Southern gateway to the Broads National Park" – is

Oulton Marshes

in Suffolk, on the Western outskirts of Lowestoft, and is a busy boating and watersports centre with a good range of amenities. The Broad itself is surrounded by nature reserves and wilderness, as you head inland, and is hence a great place to observe nature, whether by walking, hiring a boat, or joining a cruise. Adjacent to the busy quayside area of Oulton Broad is the Nicholas Everitt Park which has at least two distinctions. One is the Lowestoft Museum located in the historic Broad House. It houses, amongst other items, a fascinating collection of archaeological finds from local sites, and a fine collection of C18th Lowestoft porcelain. The other is a powerful mural by the artist Banksy, "We are all in the same boat", on a bridge in the park. It mysteriously appeared in the summer of 2021 as part of his "Spraycation" on the East coast.

Recommended Reading, Maps and Organisations relating to the Waveney Valley and wider area

1. Guide Books

Buxbaum, Tim – *Suffolk*, Shire County Guides (1996).
Knox, Margaret – *Norfolk*, Shire County Guide (1994).
Mee, Arthur – *Norfolk – The Classic Guide*. First published 1940 in the King's England series. Reissued by Amberley Publishing (2014).
Mitchell, Laurence – *Slow Norfolk and Suffolk*, Bradt (2010). Revised and reissued as *Slow Travel, Norfolk* (2014) and *Slow Travel, Suffolk* (2018).
Page, Mike – *A Broads-Eye View : The Norfolk Broads through aerial photography*, Halsgrove (2005) Also, *A Broads-Eye View 2* (2008).
Reeve, Christopher – *The Waveney Valley: History, Landscape and People*, Fonthill (2015).
River Waveney Trust – *Discover the River Waveney, from Source to Sea*, RWT (2013).
Sagar, Peter – *East Anglia: Essex, Suffolk and Norfolk*, Pallas (1994).
Skipper, Kate and Williamson, Tom – *The Angles Way: Walking in an Historic Landscape*, UEA (1993).
Start, Daniel et al – *Wild Guide: Southern and Eastern England*, Wild Things (2015).

2. Other Non Fiction, historical and nature writing – a personal selection

Bell, Adrian – *Corduroy* (1930). First in a celebrated trilogy of memoirs; *A Street in Suffolk*, Faber (1964) Occasional writings.
Cocker, Mark – *A Tiger in the Sand: Selected Writings on Nature*, Jonathan Cape (2006).
 Claxton : Field Notes from a Small Planet Vintage Books (2014).
Deakin, Roger – *Notes from Walnut Tree Farm*, Penguin (2009).
Defoe, Daniel – *A Tour through the Eastern Counties of England* (1722) Dodo Press. NB Whole text available free at Gutenberg.org.

Evans, George Ewart – *The Pattern under the Plough*, Faber (1966).
Mabey, Richard – *Nature Cure*, Pimlico (2005).
Murphy, Elaine – *Monks Hall : The History of a Waveney Valley Manor*,
   Poppyland (2018).
   Wingfield: Suffolk's forgotten castle, Poppyland (2021).
Rider Haggard, Lilias – *A Norfolk Notebook*, Faber (1946).
Sebald, W.G. – *The Rings of Saturn: An English Pilgrimage*,
   Panther (1995).

3. Maps

The Ordnance Survey (OS) Explorer maps are ideally suited to walking and outdoor activities. The scale is 1:25,000 i.e. 2.5 inches to 1 mile (4cms to 1 km). There are two that cover nearly all of the Waveney Valley, source to sea:

Explorer 230 Diss and Harleston takes in the Western stretch, from the source at Redgrave, through Diss, Harleston and beyond.

Explorer 40 The Broads covers the Eastern side, from Bungay, through Beccles to Lowestoft and Great Yarmouth.

Explorer 231 Southwold and Bungay is also useful for the Suffolk coast and inland.

Yellow Publications walking (1:16,000) and cycling (1:40,000) maps, based on OS mapping, are very handy and user friendly also, being laminated and smaller in size. They cover the whole of the UK.
   See **www.yellowpublications.co.uk** for details and coverage.

4. Local Organisations

River Waveney Trust
"The River Waveney Trust was formed in 2012 with a vision to ensure that the waters, habitats and catchment of the river are healthy for wildlife and people. We aim to achieve this by working in partnership on a range of projects which will protect, enhance and promote the river and its catchment. Projects

include natural flood management, habitat creation, river restoration, reducing pollution, improving public access and education."
www.riverwaveneytrust.org   Email **info@riverwaveneytrust.org**

Waveney Heritage Centre "Giving our past a future"
A community archives and heritage group, with a regular programme of events.
The Old School,
Grove Rd,
Brockdish, Diss,
Norfolk IP21 4JP.
www.waveneyheritage.org
Tel. **01379 668285** or **01379 669057**.

Waveney and Blyth Arts "Creatively connecting people with place along the Norfolk/Suffolk border".
WBA "promotes the distinct cultural identity of this beautiful area of N. Suffolk and S. Norfolk through exciting arts projects and events."
www.waveneyandblytharts.com
Email **info@waveneyandblytharts.com**

Norfolk Wildlife Trust was founded in 1926, and is the oldest of all the national wildlife trusts. It manages more than 50 nature reserves and protected sites, including 9 National Nature Reserves and 26 SSSI's.
www.norfolkwildlifetrust.org.uk

Suffolk Wildlife Trust was founded in 1961 and manages 60 nature reserves, most of them open to the public. 4 of these are National Nature Reserves, and 31 SSSI's.
www.suffolkwildlifetrust.org

Acknowledgements
This book is dedicated to all those organisations and individuals, in this locality and beyond, who are working to safeguard our distinctive landscapes, flora, fauna and historic buildings for the benefit of future generations. Particular thanks to the following for valued assistance and support in the preparation of the book: Alex Batho at Countryside Books; Aspa Palamidas, who also took the photographs on pages 15, 78, 84, 92 and 93 (all other photographs are by the author) and Robin Frampton.